# High Performance Selling

Advice, Tactics, and Tools.
The Complete Guide
to Sales Success

by Terry Beck

CAREER
PRESS
Franklin Lakes, NJ

HIGH PERFORMANCE SELLING
Edited by Dianna Walsh
Typeset by John J. O'Sullivan
Cover design by Barry Littman
Printed in the U.S.A. by Book-mart Press

To order this title, please call toll-free 1-800-CAREER-1
(NJ and Canada: 201-848-0310) to order using VISA or MasterCard,
or for further information on books from Career Press.

CAREER
PRESS

The Career Press, Inc., 3 Tice Road, PO Box 687,
Franklin Lakes, NJ 07417
**www.careerpress.com**

## Library of Congress Cataloging-in-Publication Data

Beck, Terry, 1962-
    High performance selling by Terry Beck.
      p. cm.
    Includes index.
    ISBN 1-56414-552-2 (paper)
      1. Selling. I. Title.

    HF5438.25 .B397 2001
    658.85—dc21

                               00-069663

# Acknowledgments

To Stacey…you're always the reason I get there.
…still falling …t.

*"You get by with a little help from your friends."*

I would like to acknowledge my family, friends, and business associates who helped me take this book from nifty idea to completed project. Notably, I would like to thank:

Cindy Johnston, Daryl Papoushek, Neil Rackham, Tom Lang, Jocelyn Williams, Bell Canada, Chris Aiken, Rob Abel, Carroll Beck, Danielle Russella, Ed Cunicelli, Mark McCleary, Mike Holloway, Jim Clarke, Basil Beck, Bell Mobility, Maureen Harvey, William Grove, Greg Harris, Chantal Sirois, Julie Boucher, Momentum Systems, Barb Hackendorn, Xerox Canada, Karen Hayward, Jim Muzyka, Roddie Davidson, Dick Comer, Larry Warnock, Documentum, Albert Ianacci, Jacqueline Feeley, Linda Davila Sheftel, Mike Miles, Miller Heiman, Inc., Jenny Johnston, Scott Cook, and Sue Dezwart.

I would also like to express my sincerest thanks to my editor, Don Loney, for his patience, understanding, and diligence over the past year, as this project slowly took form and came to life. Thanks, Don.

Finally, special thanks to Steve Pawlick and Ken Gravelle, two great leaders at Xerox who helped me learn what sales is all about.

# Contents

# Part

# Selling

# 1. The Sale Is Waiting

*". . . the customer still hasn't called me back!"*

Let me tell you about a friend of mine. He's a nice guy, but a lousy salesman. He's not new to sales, so you can't blame it on a lack of experience. He knows his stuff, so you can't blame it on a lack of knowledge. He's not low on sales talent, so you can't blame it on a lack of finesse or skill. In fact, on paper this guy packs a formidable punch. He's got a wealth of experience. He's clever, personable, well educated, and articulate. He's good with customers over the phone and in person. And yet, without even looking at his sales results—which are dismal—it's easy to spot his weakness. Or is it? Can you identify the problem here?

Let me describe the situation for you. This friend of mine arrives punctually at work every day. He sits down at his desk, logs on to his computer, returns his e-mail, responds to marketing leads. Overall, I would have to say that he writes a pretty nice proposal; he does a good job at coordinating meetings; he thinks about his approach; talks to other sales reps about strategy. He knows when to get our technical resources involved in the sale. He knows our product. He seems to have a lot of contacts. And he really knows a lot about business. He's always giving me great ideas about who knows whom, and how I might get my foot in the door with an important company in my territory.

## So what's the problem?

Let me give you a clue. When I asked him, *"What do you think is the main reason that your pipeline is poor?"* (in sales, the "pipeline" is a common metaphor for the number of sales opportunities that a salesperson is working on), his response was, *"We need a better marketing approach. I'm just not getting enough well-qualified leads."*

## What does that tell you?

It tells me that my friend will never be a success in sales, because he's waiting for the customer to come to him. I tell you this story because my friend is not alone. There are thousands—in fact, millions—of unsuccessful salespeople out there. No, let me change that to millions of unsuccessful *people*. Period. They're all out there, just waiting for something to happen. A big sale. A promotion. A larger house. A winning lottery ticket. A better job. A better life.

Which brings me to the main idea of this first chapter, an idea that deserves to be presented first, because it stands way out in front and wraps around everything else I have to say to you. We're talking about the *true meaning of selling* here, folks. A concept that is centered on the power of the individual. The power of one. And here it is:

*You don't wait for the sale. The sale waits for you.*

In fact, the whole world is out there waiting for you! Have you ever noticed that your friends, the ones who are stuck in dead-end jobs or depressed because things just "aren't working out the way they thought they would," are all *waiting* for something to happen? What is it they're waiting for? What's going to magically appear and land on their laps? Maybe they're used to support from their families. Maybe they're counting on friends to bail them out. But are parents or friends going to offer them better jobs? Or better lives? I highly doubt it. And if not, who's going to do it?

Which brings me back to my friend. He's also waiting for something to land in his lap. He's waiting for the marketing group to attract customers to his phone, and you know what? It doesn't work that way. If it did, marketing people would be making all the money. But they don't. Salespeople make all the money. And why do you suppose that is? Because salespeople are the ones who make things happen, that's why.

Do you know what I look for when I interview potential salespeople? I look for people who have gone out and done something, without waiting to be told what to do. Perhaps they've won a contest at work, or taken on a volunteer project because they believed in it, or put the big "C" on their sports jersey because leading their school team just came naturally to them. These are the kinds of people who are going to be successful. These are the kinds of people who don't wait for something to happen. It's not in their nature. They're driven to succeed. And I love that.

So, what about you? Are you the kind of person who takes the initiative? Do you take control? Would you call yourself proactive? If the answer is yes, then you've probably got what it takes to succeed in sales.

In conclusion, let me say that this is a really basic idea. But in sales, it is the foundation of what we do. You will not be successful waiting for customers to call you. Quite simply, they won't call you, because they are too busy answering calls from salespeople who really want their business—who want it badly enough to go out and get it. Don't wait for the world to beat a path to your door. Go out and get the sale.

# 2. Not Everyone in Sales Can Sell

*"Our sales reps make a ton of money, and what do they do for it? They sit by the phone and take orders. Anyone can do that!"*

Let's be clear on this from the start.

Answering the phone and taking down an order *is not selling*.

Sitting by the cash register and smiling at customers *is not selling*.

Showing your "wares" and haggling over the price *is not selling*.

And more to the point: Visiting a big corporate client and introducing yourself as the executive account manager and then sitting down over coffee to tell them about your new and fully integrated "solutions" *is most definitely not selling*.

But—

Answering the phone and digging a little deeper—now we're getting somewhere.

Walking away from the cash register and showing interest in customers—a positive sign.

Asking questions before showing anyone your product or service—now that's the ticket.

And, of course, visiting a big corporate client, introducing yourself as the executive account manager, and then sitting down over coffee to understand the client's organization and their business issues—now, *that's selling.*

Are you a seller?

# 3. Sellers Sell and Peddlers Tell

*"You've got really good presentation skills! Have you ever thought about going into sales?"*

The easiest way to tell a seller from a peddler is to watch how they engage in conversation. A seller will ask questions and listen to the responses. Through this approach, the seller will first *understand* a person's point of view and *then* make statements to address that point of view. By contrast, a peddler doesn't need, or want, to reach an understanding. Peddlers press a particular point of view—their own. They skip the questions and focus on statements. A peddler wants to be *understood*. It is this basic premise that separates sellers from peddlers.

So, why would someone choose to peddle? If you have:

- a very low price, or
- a unique product or service, or
- just a lot of really neat or new product features.

It may be appropriate to just *tell* everybody about it, on the assumption that someone is going to listen. For example, many peddlers do their telling on mass media such as television or the Internet.

So then, why should someone sell instead of peddle? If you are:

- selling a premium (you're more expensive than the competition), or

- you're not "perceived" as all that unique or special, or
- the buying organization is "complex" (many stakeholders that can say "yes" or "no" to you)...you need to sell, not tell.

That's because you need to *understand* the complexity of the buying organization before you can offer the customer a "solution" that *is different* from other offerings and *valuable enough* to justify a higher price tag.

This isn't easy to do, but who ever said that selling was easy?

In summary:

Sellers ask and listen. Peddlers talk.

Sellers win because of quality. Peddlers win because of quantity.

Sellers solve problems. Peddlers "spray" and "pray."

Which is the better approach for you? Selling or peddling?

# 4. Selling Skills Are for Life

*"I didn't trust that guy. It felt like he was trying to sell me something."*

Isn't it true that salespeople are manipulative, aggressive, dishonest, fast-talking crooks? Yes, some are. However, you may be happy to know that there is simply no evidence to support that being a jerk somehow makes you more successful. I have searched for such evidence—some study or report—that would reveal the important selling advantage that comes from being obnoxious or dishonest. I didn't find it. But what I did find was a rather substantial body of research indicating that salespeople are most successful when they learn how to:

- research, plan, and organize
- capture someone's interest
- understand and influence people
- understand business issues
- create and/or uncover business needs
- position themselves against competition
- make things happen, and
- build lasting relationships.

*Imagine the impact of those skills on the rest of your life!*

I've stumbled across an interesting trait among highly successful business people. In casual conversation, I have found that almost every one of them has been a salesperson at some point in their career. Oddly enough, many have told me that becoming a salesperson was *not* a move of their choosing or desire. In fact, fearing the negative stereotypes associated with sales and salespeople, many dreaded their first day on the job. But what I find the most interesting is that these same people have told me that the lessons learned in sales were lessons that accelerated their growth and success in almost every avenue of their personal and professional lives; lessons that helped them work with all kinds of people, in all kinds of difficult and challenging situations. And these lessons still guide them each and every day. Food for thought.

# Part  2

## Ask and Listen

# 5. Stop Talking

*"Could you believe that guy? He just wouldn't shut up!"*

Think about the last conversation that you really enjoyed. I bet that the person (or people) with whom you were speaking did a few important things:

- asked you meaningful questions that made you think,
- truly listened to your point of view, without interrupting, and
- remembered details from past events and conversations.

Good sales calls are a lot like good conversations—everybody likes to be heard!

On the other hand, we've all been caught in a conversation with someone who just wouldn't stop talking. As a society, we have become masters at tuning those people out and escaping them. We smile, nod our heads occasionally, and maybe even laugh—despite the fact that we're not listening to a single word. So think about this: If *you're* doing all the talking, what do you think your customers are doing?

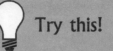
**Try this!**

Have an associate (or manager) sit in on one of your sales calls and ask them to keep an eye on the flow of conversation. After the call, ask your associate for some feedback: "Who was the focal point of the conversation? Me or my customer?" If the answer is "You," ask for specific examples of when you were talking too much, and while you're at it, get some coaching. Think: "What could I be doing differently to shift the talking emphasis to my customer, and what effect would that have on the sales call?"

## IN REVIEW

Dominating the conversation is not going to help you sell anything. Customers want to be heard. When it comes to your sales calls, you should be talking *less* than your customers.

# 6. Ask Good, Short Questions

*"Help me understand something here ..."*

If you've never had the opportunity to watch a movie featuring the detective Lieutenant Frank Columbo (starring Peter Falk), go and rent one at your local video store. Columbo is the consummate salesman when it comes to the art of asking questions. Why? Because he never has to "tell" anybody *what* the crime was or *who* did it. Or, for that matter, *why!* Columbo doesn't rely on his clever wit or knack for deductive reasoning. In fact, he often confuses his suspects with his quirky or even inept behavior. But look a little closer. Carefully concealed within his crooked back, rumpled trench coat, and weathered cigar are two incredible gifts—*a natural curiosity and a flair for asking good, short questions!*

Through his artful use of questions, he gets the bad guys to "paint themselves into a corner" and confess it all, often without even realizing it. Columbo doesn't have to figure out a thing. He just asks clear and concise questions, listens, takes a few notes, and then smacks the cuffs on!

*"I'm not sure I understand. Could you explain exactly what happened here tonight?"*

*"But if that's true, what did he do with the body?"*

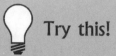 **Try this!**

First, go to your local video store, and rent a Columbo movie (my personal favorite is Murder by the Book). Now, I challenge you to come up with five short "curiosity" questions that could apply to any of your target customers (and that Columbo would be proud of). Obviously, you are not looking to solve a murder here, but you are looking to make a sale. Therefore, the goal of each question is to get your customer talking in detail about problems in their operation—problems that your product or service will fix and that will lead you to a sale. Your customers will not be confessing a crime, per se, but in effect they will be telling you about how they need your product or service—and that's powerful stuff when it comes from the customer!

*"Yes, but why would the killer care?"*

*"Really? Why's that?"*

*"How could that be?"*

And, of course, the classic:

*"Well, there is just one last thing, if it wouldn't be too much trouble. Could you tell me what you were doing last night?"*

Never underestimate the power of good, short questions!

## In Review

Tap into your Columbo skills. Ask simple and short questions to help you understand the issues that your product or service will fix.

# 7. Use Your Natural Curiosity to Get the Answers

*"If you're going to make it in this business, you have to learn how to ask the tough questions!"*

Hey, let's face it. Some questions are hard to ask. For example, when you need to:

- get inside a customer's decision-making process
- get customers to reveal information about critical issues that might actually be a little embarrassing for them
- get customers to tell you about their perception of you and your company (in the light of a few bad service situations in recent months).

And, the granddaddy of them all:

- asking for a level of commitment to move a significant sale forward.

This is not easy stuff. You don't want to blow it, right?

Here's a suggestion. Use your natural curiosity to draw out the information that you need. Avoid the interrogator's style. And here's the difference: Interrogation-type questions are typically "closed" (meaning that they can be answered with a yes, a no, or a one-word response). For example: *Are you the decision-maker?*

Ouch! I always dreaded asking questions like that. These closed-ended questions are risky. You wonder: Is it too early to ask? Have I earned the right? Does my customer want me in that close? Will they feel threatened? Isn't it too easy for them to say no and walk away?

At the very least, closed-ended interrogation-style questions are not conducive to a good conversation. Sellers who use too many closed questions have sales calls that tend to sound more like interviews punctuated by forced and awkward dialog.

Consider using instead the curious question: *How are decisions made in this organization?*

By contrast, curious questions are "open." They let your customer give more than a one-word response, and therefore you obtain much more valuable information than interrogation-type questions. You also take the edge off the question by not putting your customer in the hot seat. You are simply leading an open conversation about their situation. Here's another example:

- Interrogation question: "It looks like your photocopier is being serviced frequently. That must be aggravating your staff, is that right?"
- Curiosity question: "How's the service on your photocopier? How is that affecting your staff? Take me back to the last time it was an issue … what happened?"

But there is so much more to the art of curiosity. If you happen to be gifted with natural curiosity, you will ask questions that will help open up lines of communication. You will, with your customers' help, get a clear idea of what their business is about and what the real issues are.

Thoughtful questions about your customers' business will also reveal to you the true nature of "business" itself. The answers to your questions will help you understand how the business world works, what gets in the way, and what you can do about it.

Personally, in this process I have noticed that an interesting bond develops between curious salespeople and customers. Why? Because customers very often like to talk about their business, and curious people are eager to listen and understand. That makes for a good combination.

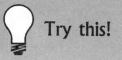

## Try this!

Below are three closed, interrogation-type questions that beg to be changed into open, curious ones. Give them a whirl; try to change them in a way that would make them easy for your customers to respond to.

1. Are you looking at competition?
2. Isn't your productivity poor?
3. Wouldn't you be happier if the system was fault-tolerant?

You'll learn about business processes and priorities. You'll get inside business structure, management process, profit and loss, competitive strategies, marketing approaches, and so much more. You'll learn about the business landscape: who the players are, who's on the way up or out. You'll learn about who's buying from whom, and who's buying whom. Every merger and acquisition will have its place in the landscape.

You'll learn about success, and about why stock prices go up. You will begin to understand why a CEO would sell off a division only to buy another one a week later. You will even learn why the subtle union of two companies can shake up an entire industry.

All of this information is out there waiting for you—waiting in the offices of your customers. And as a salesperson, you have ready access to all this information through the artful use of questions. My sales manager, Steve, used to say that the sales division of Xerox was one of the few places where you were paid to learn about business—something he called the "street-smart M.B.A."

Finally, natural curiosity will do something that no closed question could ever hope to do. It will open up opportunities that you never even considered. Since you are letting the customer talk, there is every likelihood that they will think of something that you hadn't. And that something may lead you to a big sale—one you could not have anticipated.

*Seek to understand with open, curious questions.*

## IN REVIEW

Open, curiosity questions are relatively easy to ask of your customers and help to build your relationships with them. You also can obtain a lot of valuable information. Valuable because it can lead you to a sale.

# 8. When in Doubt, Ask Your Customer

*"Do you think they're looking at the competition?"*

I get asked for my opinion on many selling topics, such as:

- How long should a proposal be?
- How do you know when the customer is in the buying window?
- How do you know if a customer values a relationship?
- How do you know if the customer will do business with us?
- How do you know if the customer is looking at your competition?

I often smile when I hear those questions because I remember myself wondering the same sorts of things early in my sales career. In those days, I assumed that a big part of selling was a guessing game. You spent a lot of time trying to figure out what your customer was thinking and then you hoped like hell that you were right! Unfortunately, I found myself thinking and saying things like:

- Geez, I thought that Bob was the ultimate decision-maker. I didn't even know he had a boss.

  or

- They bought from our competitor because the client had the same kind of system in her other office. How was I supposed to know?

or even worse

- They just didn't like our proposal. It was too long and confusing!

In all three cases I could have uncovered critical information, and saved the sale, if only I had asked the customer a question, instead of making my own assumption. For example:

- Bob, who makes the ultimate decision on this one?
- Do you have a preference for any one vendor?
- What would you like to see in our proposal?

Unfortunately, those questions don't exactly "roll off the tongue" in casual conversation. They can be difficult questions to ask. I've heard many a sales manager refer to them as the "tough questions." I can even recall one conversation when the sales manager said to his rep, "Well, that's all very interesting, but did you ask the 'tough question' at the end of the call?" They're tough because they're very direct and we may not get the answer we desire. But I say, so what? It doesn't change the fact that you need to know, so my simple advice to you is resist the urge to guess, or ask for an opinion from your boss or sales associate. Get it straight from the horse's mouth.

*If it's important customer information you're after—ask your customer.*

# 9. Assume Nothing

*"I'm sure it's between us and one other competitor!"*

Assumptions are the Achilles' heel of the sales rep!

We talk about our accounts as if they really are "our" accounts. We proudly display our knowledge of their business, their needs, their decision process, their world. How often, though, is the information that comes from our mouths based on an assumption? How often do we make an inference or a leap of faith on the basis of an observation or just our own intuition—our "gut feeling," if you will. I've been guilty of this.

I remember one account in particular. I was convinced that the sale was ready to close in November one year. But my convictions were not based on tangible facts. Rather, I got the closing "feeling" from some assumptions that I had made; assumptions that were based on some piecemeal information I had collected over a short period of time. I felt *good* about the sale, but when push came to shove I couldn't back that feeling up with any hard data. You can probably guess the outcome. (It was delayed eight months from the day I thought it would close!)

Here are some real-life examples—examples of some classic assumptions that have brought sales cycles to a standstill:

- He assumed the customer was ready to look at a proposal…they were just curious about the technology.
- She assumed the customer needed a demo…they would have bought without it.
- They assumed the proposal would be very detailed…the decision-maker who had to read it hates detail.
- They assumed the executive assistant is just a screen to be avoided…the boss does nothing without her okay.
- We assumed that it's between us and the other premium vendor…there's a third low-cost provider coming on strong.
- They assumed the decision will be made by the end of the quarter…the customer has no budget yet.
- We assumed they will go with us if the price is right…the customer is using our proposal to drive down the price of a competitor—the one she really wants to do business with!
- She assumed Mr. Big is the decision-maker…he isn't, and will only pass it to another individual who doesn't know the slightest thing about her company or her proposal.
- He assumed the sale is won...the sale was lost two weeks ago!

How many sales have I lost because of my clever assumptions? Too many!

Assumptions are doubly dangerous thanks to the current pace of change. Even if we keep our facts straight, even if we have flushed out the real situation through exhaustive investigation and research—look out! The world keeps spinning, and it doesn't take long for your sales situation to do an abrupt about-face when you're not looking. How many times has your own company made changes to its decision-making process, for example? It's getting so difficult to keep up that many companies don't bother publishing "official" organization charts any more because they're out of date by the time they are printed.

While assumptions are deadly and pervasive, there is a simple solution. When you think you have the facts straight, ask yourself this question: *Do I really know this to be true or am I just guessing?* If

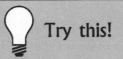

## Try this!

This exercise is for salespeople who have to fill out account plans. Account plans are detailed and often lengthy documents that outline valuable information about the customer (the players, business objectives, decision-making process, etc.), so that the entire account team can be well informed, moving in the same direction, and aligned with common goals. Typically, account plans are completed for the largest and highest-profile accounts.

you have even the shadow of a doubt, go to the source—ask your customer!

I would now ask you to retrieve one and take it with you to your next call with the customer concerned.

At the beginning of the call, introduce the idea of an account plan, its purpose, and its benefit for the customer (i.e., "It will help our account team to stay focused on your changing needs, and it will help us avoid those annoying redundancies caused by account teams who are not working in concert").

Now ask the customer to help you complete an empty account plan, as though you had never completed it yourself.

When the call is over, find a quiet corner to compare the two account plans—your initial plan, based on your assumptions, and your collaborative plan, based on actual (and current) customer input.

If you've done a good job avoiding assumptions, the account plans should be similar. If you've assumed too much, then this exercise is a good way of giving you a reality check. At the very least, you may learn something about the account (customers have an odd way of being very frank when they are recording something for posterity) that will be useful to you and your team.

# In review

Assumptions are easy to make and can just as easily backfire on you. Unfortunately, today's corporate selling environment is changing so fast that assumptions have become doubly dangerous. Without having your finger on the customer's pulse, you could be positioning and working towards an opportunity that doesn't exist. If you don't know, don't guess; and don't rely on old information. Do yourself a favor: If there's any doubt in your mind, ask the customer.

# Part

## Rules of Thumb

# 10. The Buying Cycle Is More Important than the Selling Cycle

*"What really gets me is that he knows it's my month-end, and he hasn't even looked at the proposal yet ..."*

Ask sales reps to identify their favorite stage of the "selling cycle," and they'll be happy to oblige. Ask them to identify their favorite stage of the "buying cycle," and they will probably give you a funny look. That's unfortunate. The truth is, sellers' ability to understand and influence the buying cycle is infinitely more important than their understanding of their selling cycle. Why? *Because buyers are the ones who buy, that's why.*

Let me give you an example. If you go to your customer to *explore needs* (a step in the selling cycle that all sales reps know about), but you fail to recognize that your customer is *shopping for a solution* (a step in their buying cycle) to satisfy needs that they have already identified, there is a good chance that your customer will get annoyed by your probing questions. ("Why do you keep asking me these questions? What I need is a solution to my problem!")

If you are in the *closing stage* (selling cycle), but your customer hasn't finished *shopping* (buying cycle), then you are going to annoy the customer by your attempts to close the sale, and will likely get a dreaded objection such as "I'd like to think about it."

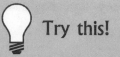 Try this!

Here's a quick test. Take a look at your "prospect bank," "sales funnel," or whatever you call the list of the customers who you think will buy from you in the foreseeable future.

On a copy of that list draw a column with the heading "Customer's Stage." Go down your prospect list and enter one of the following descriptions in the column you have just created:

1. Status quo—for those customers who do not see the need for change ("Everything's A-OK").

2. Evaluating problem(s)—for those customers who recognize that there are issues that you can solve, but are not yet committed to doing anything about them (they're not in the buying window).

3. Fixing problems—for those customers who recognize the problem(s) and have begun to allocate time and money to fixing it (them). In other words, these customers are committed and have moved into the buying window.

4. Shopping for solutions—for those customers who are committed and are looking at different ways to solve their problems—that is, looking at proposals from you and your competitors.

5. Working out details—for those customers who are narrowing the field by creating a short list of acceptable solutions and/or suppliers. The customer is now working towards final approval.

This assignment is a tricky task, so be careful about which stage you choose. For example, customers who put out a Request for Proposal (RFP) may seem to fit stage 4, "Shopping for solutions," but often I have found that RFPs were just fact-finding missions. These customers just wanted to kick the tires, as it were. They were not really serious about fixing their problems, but only fishing for ideas. Therefore, these "fishing expeditions," as we called them, meant that the customer was in stage 2, "Evaluating the problem," because they had not yet decided that it was time to commit their resources (stage 3). That's a long-winded example of this idea: Resist the urge to fill in what you think you should. Analyze the situation for what it is. Put yourself in the shoes of your customer: "Where is my customer in their decision process?"

When you have completed the assignment, compare your findings to your original list. If you are like me, there are prospects on your list who really are not committed and, therefore, are not true prospects. Do yourself a favor and get them off the list, or get out of there and sell them.

Forget about your sales cycle for a minute and consider: "Where is my customer?"

## IN REVIEW

You should be more concerned with your customer's stage in their buying process than you are with your stage in your selling process. Why? Because customers are the ones who buy—that's why.

# 11. There's No Such Thing As a Typical Day

*"Another well-planned day shot to hell!"*

I am now going to illustrate a typical day in the life of a professional salesperson.

The typical day begins with ... well, let me put it another way. Traditionally, salespeople have begun the day, by ... okay, let's skip the introduction. Let me just outline a typical day for you, rather than discuss the details. So, as an outline, the average day of a salesperson, in my opinion, or as presented by me, is as follows ... Let's back this up and try again, shall we? Perhaps I should use a graphic. No, that wouldn't work. Okay, so here it is, ladies and gentlemen, I give you "The Typical, Predictable Day" ...

This isn't working.

There's just no getting around it. No day in the life of a professional salesperson ever looks like the one before, and it will look that much different again by the time tomorrow rolls around. So, what are we saying here? I guess if you have your heart set on enjoying a "typical" day—one that has a predictable series of events from daybreak to sunset—or one that at least gets you into a comfortable routine—I have just one suggestion: Stay out of sales!

# 12. Keep It Short and Simple—The KISS Principle

*"Did you understand what that sales rep was talking about?"*

In my experience, the wisest people choose the fewest words to describe something: "A fool and his money are soon parted."

That's because people who really know their stuff find it relatively easy to express their thoughts and ideas in words that everyone can understand. People who don't know their stuff, or are trying to impress you with their knowledge, will often take the simplest messages and make them complicated or long-winded: "A person lacking the essential wherewithal to conduct themselves wisely will often make questionable value judgments concerning financial matters and overall fiscal policy that produce undesirable results in a relatively short time frame."

Customers have discovered this selling truth, and will become quickly annoyed by long-winded sales reps who don't know what they're talking about, or are just trying to sound good. Don't kid yourself—customers are too busy and too distracted to make sense of your "sales talk."

If you have a message to get across, "Keep it short and simple" (KISS). Make it easy for your clients to understand you and they will relate more easily to you. Sales reps who have mastered the KISS principle have customers who say: "Her solution really made sense to us!"

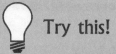 **Try this!**

Pick a friend (or family member) who knows little about your product or service. Practice making a ten-minute product and/or service presentation to this person, highlighting your key competitive strengths. There should be no interruptions. Before you begin, ask your audience to make a mental note when the presentation gets confusing, complicated, and/or long-winded. When you've finished your presentation, review the list. Make adjustments to your presentation and try it again.

My challenge to you: Can you shave 25 percent off your presentation time on your second attempt? If you've followed the KISS principle, it should be easy!

## IN REVIEW

When talking or writing, choose words that are short, simple, and easy to understand.

# 13. Ditch the Pitch

*"He actually said that he needed to talk to his sales manager. I can't believe they still use that line."*

Why is it that salespeople have to reinforce negative stereotypes by resorting to "cheesy" sales talk?:

- We've bought the whole shipment and are passing the savings on to you.
- This is a limited-time offer!
- I'll have to talk to my manager about that.
- That's funny, we've never had a problem with service before!
- It's foolproof!
- Don't worry about installation, it's a no-brainer.

These phrases are more than just annoying—they pose a major threat to the credibility of the sales reps who use them. Most customers are educated people and most educated people don't like to be conned. Bottom line? When you hear somebody talking like a hustler, there is a tendency to believe they *are* a hustler.

Don't try to be tricky. Talk to your customers the way you would talk to anyone else.

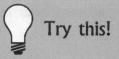 Try this!

Sit in on an associate's sales presentation. Whenever the associate uses sales lingo, take a look at the face of the customer. Categorize their reaction under "impressed," "indifferent," or "annoyed." Review your analysis following the presentation and judge for yourself.

## In review

Sales lingo confuses and annoys customers and, what is worse, often erodes the customer-seller relationship.

# 14. Set Expectations for Your Sales Meeting

*"Okay. So why are we all here today?"*

I get a kick out of sales meetings that just sort of "begin" without a beginning. Those are the same meetings that seem to meander off-track, much to the dismay of those stuck in the room. In those situations, I find it common, if not predictable, that meeting participants become increasingly confused and agitated as the seconds tick by. Observe as they glance nervously at their watches, tap their pens on the table, or stare blankly into space. I imagine them thinking:

- *Where is this going?*
- *Just what are we talking about?*
- *Why did I agree to this? I've got to get out of here!*

These meetings often end as they begin, without any real conclusions or meaningful next steps; and, while it may surprise you, I am amazed at the number of sales calls that have been conducted in exactly this manner. A sales call opens with light conversation and draws to a close with no real return on investment—no actions or agreements, just a collection of scribbled notes on a whiteboard and a mad dash for the door.

What a waste of time!

Try looking at a sales call as another type of meeting where you are responsible for its success. Let me repeat: The responsibility for the outcome rests with you—the seller. Here are some suggestions to en-

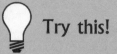

## Try this!

Prior to your next sales call, write down an agenda with the help of the six-step process outlined in this chapter: purpose/ expectations/agenda/discussion/ review/action plan. Before you begin writing your agenda, think about the desired outcome of that sales call: What do you want to accomplish? What is the return on investment for you and for your customer?

sure that your call is not cataloged under the "What just happened?" or "What a complete waste of time" categories:

1.  Start by reviewing the *purpose* of the meeting (that is, why are you there?).
2.  Get everyone's meeting *expectations* out on the table by asking, "What would make this meeting a good use of your time?"
3.  Agree on an *agenda* based on those expectations.
4.  Lead the *discussion*.
5.  *Review* the outcomes of the discussion and ask, "Have your expectations been met?"
6.  And finally, put a manageable action plan in place before everyone leaves!

My bet is that your meeting skills, on their own merits, will build confidence and credibility with your customers. Following one of my own sales calls, I have actually had a customer say to me, "That was a really productive meeting. I wish my staff meetings were that organized!"

## IN REVIEW

When it comes time to conduct a sales call, find out what your customer expects before you begin. If you want a solid return on investment for both you and your customer, it helps to be well organized and to have your plan in place.

# 15. There's a Way to Solve Problems

*"What are my options here?"*

Imagine that you are the vice-president of sales. You're an approachable person, right? Imagine you are so approachable that you create an open-door policy at your company—anyone who has an issue can walk right into your office and talk to you about it. Wouldn't that be nice? Your employees would love you for it. But watch out. In my experience, employees at every level love to vent their problems, especially to a boss who's willing to listen. That means you're going to spend a lot of time listening to people who love to complain.

But what if one of your best sales reps, Carrie, were to walk into your office to present a problem and then propose a solution? Wouldn't that be refreshing? I bet she would earn your respect on that day, right?

Welcome to the art of problem-solving. It's not an easy art to master, because complaining about problems is just so much easier than fixing them. How do I know that? Because I used to be a chronic complainer. I would march right up to my manager the instant something went wrong and let him have it in no uncertain terms. Fortunately, I have worked for a few excellent managers in my day, and one in particular, Ken, patiently taught me that "reacting" to problems doesn't really do anybody any good. And that's what complaining really amounts to—it's just a negative reaction to something we don't like.

I never heard Ken complain. Not once. Ken was a problem-solver, and his secret was twofold. First, he didn't react to anything! In fact, Ken personified grace under pressure. Even when it seemed that the whole department was falling down around him, Ken would sit with his arms crossed listening to the complainer drone on and on about the horror of it all. Second, Ken had a process that he would apply to each and every problem brought into his office. When the complainer stopped complaining, Ken would unfold his arms and take the problem apart, piece by piece, and then put together a solution from the best options available to him. That's called "problem-solving," and Ken consistently applied that same model to everybody's difficulties.

Ken's model was a real bonus for me personally. Because I am a very spontaneous person, I had found myself reacting too quickly, and with too much emotion, when things went wrong. Ken's model forced me to think first and act second. I found that I was able to distance myself from the emotion of the moment, simply by letting my analytical side take over. I can tell you that, when I give myself the chance to use my head first, my problem-solving effectiveness quadruples.

Another big benefit of Ken's model is that problems *get* solved. Since the model taught me to think about solutions, rather than react to problems, I found myself tackling issues head-on, which stopped little problems from festering and becoming bigger and more annoying.

Do you think you could benefit from Ken's approach? Do you find yourself reacting irrationally when a big problem crops up? If so, consider his model. Here's a condensed version of the steps Ken follows when his complainers have finished complaining:

## KEN'S PROBLEM-SOLVING MODEL
1. What's the problem?
2. What's the root cause of the problem?
3. What options are available to fix the root cause?
4. What's our best option?

Sounds pretty simple, doesn't it? But how do you apply the model to the infamous "real world"?

## Applying the problem-solving model

Here's a real-world example. Let's go back to our opening scenario where you are the vice-president of sales. Let's say you are sitting in your office, reflecting on your long day of employee complaints (remember that open-door policy?). Lately the complaints have been focused on the sales order– approval process. First, the sales reps have been walking in your door and complaining that there are too many errors in the order approval process, and that these errors are delaying product installation. And that means customers are unhappy. It also means that commissions are delayed, so the sales reps aren't happy, either. Second, you've also had to listen to the order administration team, who are sick of hearing sales reps complain to them about delays and are also fed up with an order system that they say is too old and cumbersome to keep up with changes to the order paperwork.

Well, remember Carrie, the problem-solver? Here she comes again:

Mr. Johnson, sorry to bother you, but we have a *problem* that is preventing our sales orders from getting processed quickly. We can't seem to get order paperwork through the system in less than a week and that's really slowing things down. Now, I've talked to Ginny in order admin and a few of the other reps, so here's what I think is the *root cause*. Basically, the paperwork has too much room for interpretation, and therefore way too much room for error. Every order we create is slightly different from the one before, which means that Ginny's staff is manually reviewing every order processed. And that takes way too much time.

As I see it, we have a couple of *options*. First, we can keep the status quo, but that means that some of our month-end sales will slip into the next month. (VPs don't like that option.) We can also have one person assigned to handle exceptions, so that anything out of the norm goes directly to that person for speedy approval. But Ginny says her group is already short on staff as it is. So here's the *best option*, as I see it. Ginny said that her team could create an order template that requires the salespeople to choose options from a menu. That way, there would be no room for interpretation, and provided we have enough menu options to accommodate the sales force, we could really speed up cycle time. What do you think?

## In review

Here's the message: Be a problem-solver. Think through every problem and your options for solving it.

# Part 4

## About You

# 16. Attitude is Everything

*"Three months in a row below quota! Sales sucks!"*

Have you ever had to sit through a presentation that went on and on about how the secret of happiness and success is basically to "put on a happy face"? As for me, when a presentation or meeting turns into a "smiles" campaign, I create an excuse to leave the room. Why? Because I don't buy it! I think most of it is just fluff!

Does that sound harsh? If it does, I come by it honestly. I've had to sit, stand, read, watch, and otherwise listen to too many "positive attitude" speeches that spout the same thing:

- The glass is half full.
- Look on the bright side.
- Go for it!
- Realize your potential.
- Tap into your creative side.
- Reach for your dream.

Well, not to throw a wrench in the works, but I don't think it's possible for human beings to put on a happy face, if that means changing their attitudes by any significant measure! And I also don't think that being a happy or positive person is going to make you automatically more successful in sales!

How do you like them apples?

If you disagree, I would ask you to consider where I'm coming from. I would like to introduce my take on "attitude," and then apply that to my experience in selling.

Let's start with what attitude is *not*—it's not a light switch! When someone tells you that changing your attitude can be fast and relatively easy—like flicking a switch—I think they are talking about "acting," not "attitude." (See Chapter 18, "Creating a Sales Personality Is a Big Mistake.")

I believe that "attitude" is *your expression of you.* It is simply what people see on the outside to give them an indication of what's on the *inside.* You can't turn it on when and where you want because there is no easy way to activate or deactivate a lifetime of development. After all, if you accept the fact that attitude is the outward expression of ourselves, then we are talking about a very complicated expression. We are talking about the emotional construction of human beings that begins to take shape at a very young age and then evolves over years of learning, growth, and change. To sum up, you cannot easily change your attitude because you cannot easily change yourself—*you are who you are!*

In my opinion, attitude is both your genetic makeup and your life experience rolled into an action, an opinion, or a mood. It's your values, your fears, your knowledge, your beliefs, and even your culture. Attitude is more than a smile—it's every expression on your face! It's the way that you carry yourself into an office; it's your reaction in a crisis; it's your view of the situation; it's your comments on the latest change in the organization; and it's how you spend your Saturday mornings. It's your patience and control, and your capacity to accept change. It's your highest highs and your lowest lows.

And what I find particularly interesting about attitude is not how salespeople can "put on a happy face"—that's easy to fake, in the short term. Rather, what impresses me are two things: First, successful salespeople know they can and *will* make the next sale (childhood reference—*The Little Engine That Could*). Second, and arguably more important, successful salespeople do not really see failure as an option—they just don't give up.

These are the two attitudes that really matter. These are the attitudes that I have seen on the faces and in the actions of *all* highly successful salespeople, and these are the attitudes that cannot be created or changed easily:

- Attitude 1: *I will be successful!*
- Attitude 2: *I will not give up!*

And now, here's a friendly challenge to the "positive attitude" theory as it applies to salespeople. Take a second look at the successful salespeople you have met. Are they all the same? Are they all well adjusted, happy, "cup-half-full" people, with lots of energy and enthusiasm? To me, the answer is a resounding *no*. The plain and simple truth is that there is no one cookie-cutter mold. There is no super salesman or -woman with that enchanting smile and sparkling persona. In fact, I've met thousands of salespeople over the years whose personalities are unique and all over the map: insecure, obnoxious, shy, outgoing, introverted, personable, happy, dull, sarcastic, stupid, manipulative, miserable, brilliant, and crazy—and everything in between.

I will concede that within that broad group there were lots of positive and happy people, but they accounted for only part of the total. Here is the bottom line: I've known lots of unhappy and negative people who still believed in success and would not give up, and guess what? They were also highly effective sellers.

So what's the deal here? Am I just taking potshots at positive and happy people because I want to be different? No. It's just that I've reached three important conclusions about attitude:

1. You are who you are (I think this bears repeating). And what this really means is that if you've always considered yourself to be more of a realist than a member of the happy-go-lucky set, I'm here to tell you that's okay.
2. Be yourself! Don't try to change your attitude overnight, because it ain't going to work.

3.  If you've got the "right stuff"—the attitudes of "Yes, I'll be successful" and "Yes, I'm staying out of the quitters' line," I'm here to tell you that choosing a career in sales is a wise decision. If you lack these attitudes, you will have a very tough time coping with the unavoidable cycles of success and failure that accompany professional selling.

Let me conclude with an example of how the two success attitudes in sales can carry over to other areas of life. The best example I can think of comes from major league baseball. For two consecutive years, my hometown team (the Toronto Blue Jays) was the best professional baseball team in the world. Joe Carter was a pivotal player for the club in both of those years and there is an aspect of Joe's job that requires our two success attitudes. Joe gets paid to walk up to a plate and swing a bat at a ball. Success is only measured when his bat makes contact with the ball, and then only when the ball lands in certain places. Well, if you follow baseball, you know that Joe's odds of success are relatively low and, predictably, he fails in the majority of attempts. Joe is a very highly paid failure. Arguably, there are days when his entire batting game goes to pot. No hits, no walks, no runs.

Yet, when Joe is standing at the plate, he seems remarkably calm and composed, indeed, utterly focused on his job, even in the middle of a seasonal slump. How is that possible? You would think continual failure at such a simple task would turn anyone off the sport; it's so humiliating to just stand there swinging and missing (sorry, Joe). But it's possible because Joe, and other successful players like him, embrace our two attitudes of success. Adapted to baseball, they are "I know I will hit this ball eventually" and "I will not quit until I do." Thanks to both his talent and the law of averages, Joe is assured that success will come. He will continue to practice. He will continue to work hard. He is secure in the knowledge that if today doesn't work out, he will try again tomorrow. Joe will not let the negative aspects of his job—his failure to make contact with the ball—change his attitude towards the game and towards his success. His attitude helps carry him through the good and the bad.

There is a happy footnote to this story: Much to my own delight and that of all of the hometown fans, Joe's attitude was well rewarded in October of 1993 when he whacked the ball into the left-field stands for a game-winning and World Series–winning home run.

When it comes to attitude—*sales can be a lot like baseball.*

# 17. Persistence Is Also Everything

*"I have to hand it to him—he wouldn't take no for an answer!"*

My dad said a weird thing to me when I first told him that I was going to take the plunge and join the sales team at Xerox. He said, "Son, remember it's 10 percent inspiration and 90 percent perspiration." At the time, I didn't get it. (I just thought he was trying to be clever.) But after a few years in the Xerox school of hard knocks, his words began to sink in, just as the novelty of sales began to wear off. It was then that I learned an important thing about the "perspiration" part. I learned that you had to get up every day and just go for it. With this idea in mind, I would like to define what perspiration (a.k.a. persistence) means in a specific sales situation.

First, I would ask that you pick a current sales opportunity that falls under all three of the following criteria:

- You have done everything you can;
- You are waiting for the customer to do something; and
- You are ready to throw in the towel if something doesn't happen soon!

Here's my simple advice to you: *Persist!*

I'm talking about the sale that may be getting ugly, much to your shock and amazement.

I'm talking about the sale that seemed like the perfect fit—the right customer, the right solution, the right time, and the right place. No problems—until today. Now the fit doesn't seem so right.

I'm talking about the sale where you were getting strong buying signals, but now something's changed.

I'm talking about the sale that you should have won by now!

Then why accept anything less? *Persist.*

- Even if they say no...*persist*!
- Even if they stop returning your calls...*persist*!
- Even if they want to think about it...*persist*!
- Even if they just can't make up their minds...*persist*!

If you think you have done everything you can—think again! Start over and think of something new to show the customer that you believe in the sale.

- Find out why they've changed their minds!
- Make the extra phone call!
- Leave the follow-up voice mail!
- Get the extra reference!
- Write the heartfelt follow-up letter!
- Take somebody out to lunch!
- Make a new contact!
- Get somebody else's opinion!
- Camp out at their doorstep—if that's what it takes!

There will be times when your persistence alone will make the difference between winning and losing.

# 18. Creating a Sales Personality Is a Big Mistake

*"You know what your problem is? You're just too honest!"*

A funny thing happened to me on the way to a sales call. I was in the car with my sales manager when he let me in on a little secret: *"Terry, you're a nice guy, but maybe a little too nice."*

In response to my puzzled look, he went on to explain that my personal style was too straightforward. I was just too honest with customers, and that was going to be a problem in sales. Of course, this left me in a bit of a tizzy, given that we were five minutes from the sales call and my manager had just pointed out a major flaw in my personality. What was I to do?

Well, I tried very hard to be "smooth" and "slick" at that sales call. In fact, I was trying so hard to be different, that I really couldn't concentrate on anything else. In the process I tuned out the customer, the conversation, and my focus on the sale—all in an effort to come off sounding like somebody I wasn't. My sales manager basically took over the call as I sat floundering over what I should or should not be saying. It was a disaster!

But it didn't end there! I had a lot of respect for my sales manager, so I tried repeatedly to adapt my selling style according to his opinion. However, after a few more horrendous calls, I came to an important conclusion. I had better figure out a way to adapt sales to me, and not

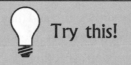 Try this!

1. Ask your manager, your trainer, or a few successful associates to describe the steps that they use when making a prospecting call.
2. When you have heard from at least three different sources, identify which steps are common to the group.
3. Write the common steps down in order (that is, the cold-calling process).
4. Using the steps as a guide, prepare a cold-calling script for a real customer whom you will be calling this month. Be sure to use the common steps, but also give it your own personal flair. Use your own thoughts and your own words. As long as you stick to the successful steps or formula, you should have no problem getting the same positive results from your own personal approach. Good luck.

me to sales. I just couldn't concentrate on selling when I was trying so hard to reconstruct myself in front of the customer. The whole experience made me realize something important about selling. If you try to be something you're not, you are an actor, not a business person. And that means you are concentrating on acting, and not business.

The other big point here is that I took it upon myself to change something that had taken me a lifetime to develop—my personality. And that just isn't easy. So my coaching tip to you is this: If someone tells you that you need to be more friendly, or more aggressive, or more persuasive, analyze the situation for what it is. Are you capable of making that change? Does it require a major shift in your personality? A departure from who you are?

If you can't easily adapt, then don't. The alternative? If you can't adapt to the change, have the change adapt to you. For example, take the prospecting call (or cold call, as it is often called). It's tempting to try and use the same words, tone, and body language as your trainer or manager. After all, they were successful, and they have given you their exact formula for success. But the truth is, they have already taken the essential components of a good prospecting call and adapted them to their personalities. So if you try to copy their content and their style, it will never work.

The trick is finding your trainers' or managers' skill *inside* their style. That means identifying the fundamentals of their approach—the steps or the process. Once you've done that, it's relatively easy to adapt the sales skill to *you*.

*Be yourself.*

## IN REVIEW

Adapt sales skills to your personality. The only sales personality you require is your own.

# 19. Chameleon Sellers Blend In

*"You're not going to wear that suit into the plant, are you?"*

Have you ever been to a traditional Japanese restaurant? Imagine the scene. Out of respect for your host, you remove your shoes. You speak in muted tones. You sit at a low table. You embrace the serenity surrounding a Japanese meal, even if it means sacrificing the comfort of a chair. You begin to understand a little of Japanese culture, even if it's just for a meal. You are, as your mom would have put it, "expanding your horizons."

With this analogy in mind, I find it unforgivable that many sales-people will walk into a customer's office *as though they own it*. They become rude and overbearing; they talk in sales-speak; they boast about their latest products, completely oblivious to their surroundings. This kind of behavior raises the question: By what right do we walk into a business environment and try to impose our way of thinking or our way of working on the client?

Consider the lowly chameleon. This clever little lizard will actually change skin color in order to blend in with its surroundings. The chameleon sales rep will essentially do the same thing by *adapting* to the customer's environment rather than trying to *dominate* it. People who respect a business environment are less likely to be viewed as a threat, and more likely to develop a partnership. Meanwhile, just down the hall, the overbearing rep is coming off as an adversary, someone who is looking for a business to conquer, not to help.

Think about *your* style. Do you adapt to the buying environment? Do you embrace your client's business? A good clue is your choice of clothing. If you are dressed to kill in your favorite Armani while paying a call on an auto parts manufacturing plant, my guess is that you have missed the boat on chameleon selling.

Give yourself this test: Pick your top three accounts and try to describe the culture of their organizations. What could you be doing to be more of the chameleon in those environments?

*Chameleons survive by blending into their environment. Their louder competitors get eaten up!*

# 20. Self-Confidence Is No Secret

*"In the end, I think it was his self-confidence that set him apart from the other sales reps. He really believed in his product."*

We have all met people who exude self-confidence from every pore. As a customer, I feel much more at ease when I'm around confident salespeople because I have found that there is a strong correlation between *confidence* and *competence*.

Imagine this situation. On your way to a sales call, you pick up an angry voice mail message and discover that the customer you are about to visit has just had a system crash—*your system*. This is a customer who is already furious about the number of crashes that have occurred recently, and you have gone on record as saying that it wouldn't happen again. I might add that all of these problems are coming to you in the middle of a big sales cycle, in which you are trying to convince this same angry customer to upgrade the system with your new mega-expensive product. And just for fun, this same customer is not only the decision-maker, but she's the one who is insisting on looking at a competitor claiming to have a far more reliable and cost-effective product. And she has never looked at the competition before!

As you listen to her chilly message, how are you feeling? (This is scary stuff!)

Well, guess what? If you are just starting your sales career, there is a 100 percent chance that a very similar situation will find you, and if you are like me, the stress level will begin to mount with every step you take towards that customer's office:

*(step...step...step) So much for that bonus check, and, for that matter, you can kiss this account goodbye. And while we're on the subject, I can't wait to hear my district manager's reaction when he learns I just lost an account that has been doing business with us for ten consecutive years. (step...step...step)*

What do you think will happen if you walk into the customer's office with your proverbial tail tucked between your legs, and your self-confidence tucked right along with it? As my mother used to say, "If you start out on the wrong foot, there's a pretty good chance you're going to finish on it!"

Worse yet, as your customer sees a new side of you—where you are at a confidence low—she will start to draw the inevitable parallels between confidence and competence. So, if you are walking into her door with your head down and a bushel full of excuses, just imagine what she is thinking:

*Hmmm, I guess these guys just aren't on top of their game anymore.*

*Whatever it is, they can't fix it.*

*Maybe they're hiding something from me.*

*All that money we're spending and the system doesn't even work.*

*I guess it's time to look at alternatives.*

No matter how you slice it, your confidence level is going to be noticed. So here's my suggestion: The next time you are about to embark on a very important sales call, imagine that your self-confidence level is a fork in the road lying between you and your customer. Going left or right will require a decision on your part:

- *The Left Fork* = HIGH self-confidence. *Decision*: Proceed to the call!
- *The Right Fork* = LOW self-confidence. *Decision*: Stop!

If you feel you are at the right fork, there must be a reason for your low self-confidence, especially if it's not the norm for you. So if you can act and begin to fix the problem, then take the time and do it now!

- Call the systems engineer to understand the exact nature of the recurring system crash.
- Call your manager, explain the problem, and ask for some advice.
- Figure out a creative way of making up for the errors— that is, an immediate application study to determine a more reliable way to run the system.
- Get the systems engineer to accompany you on the call so that you can introduce yourselves as the "problem-resolution team."
- Ask one of your best customers to call the angry customer, in an effort to assure her that this is the exception and not the rule.
- Figure out what impact the system crash is having on her business, and come up with a creative short-term solution to keep her business moving.

I have found that being brave enough to show up late with a higher confidence level—*confident because I have done something about it*—is much, much better than being on time but off the mark.

If it's a major problem and something you can't fix or do anything about immediately, reschedule or delay the meeting until your self-confidence has been restored, if you can. Why reschedule? Remember, if you carry your confidence low into an important meeting, it's very likely that your customers will be questioning your competence—and that may close a door that will be difficult to reopen.

*Customers will not knowingly buy incompetence!*

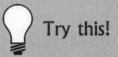 **Try this!**

Pick an account that concerns you, one that is having major service or support problems, and one that you will be visiting in the near future. Ask yourself, "What creative things can I do [see the list in this chapter] to turn this negative solution into a positive one, and at the same time, make me feel much more confident about the sale and about the account?" Then go ahead and do it!

## IN REVIEW

Self-confidence levels are detectable by your customers! Low self-confidence will affect your sales performance, your relationships with customers, and, of course, your end results. You will find that doing something about your self-confidence prior to the call is always better than just waiting around for it to get better on its own, or blowing an important call because *you just weren't up for it!*

# 21. Don't Worry About Your Hair

*"Never cross your legs like that. It sends a message to your customers that you're closed off."*

Have you ever "had your colors done"? For what it's worth, I'm an "autumn." I think that means that I look better in dark colors (but don't quote me on that). I learned about "colors" at a very fun workshop that focused on the importance of nonverbal communication in sales. The lady who ran the workshop was an expert on clothing styles, colors, facial expressions, personal hygiene, and even the right and wrong way to hold your hands and the proper way to sit in a chair during sales calls. It was actually quite entertaining, and very interesting stuff to me. Until then, I had no idea that so much rides on physical appearance and actions.

But what really surprised me that day was the reaction from the group. Here I thought we were just getting some friendly advice, but our group discussion went on for hours. It seemed that everybody had a personal testimonial about the vast importance of one's physical appearance. I actually felt kind of silly, because there were some pretty serious conversations going on about stuff that I always thought was pretty trivial. "Never lean back in your chair; your fingernails should not be too long; facial hair is an absolute no-no; keep your hands down; never jingle change in your pocket; wear this, but never that; cross your legs in this direction, but only if the client is doing the same."

I was flabbergasted. By the end of the seminar I began to worry about how many "don'ts" I was doing, and how many "dos" I had to start doing.

Well, that was a long time ago, and over the years I have learned something about nonverbal communication that I think is worth sharing. Nonverbal communication is important—but it's not *that* important! After all, you're a business person, not a model. What you wear and how you carry yourself have some importance (I mean you want to look and act like a professional, right?), but take it all with a grain of salt. The color of your suit and the way you hold your hands really doesn't amount to a hill of beans compared to making the right recommendation to your customer. It's just not that important. Period.

People will buy from you despite your odd quirks and behaviors. They'll buy from you because they trust you and they believe in your products or services. If you happen to score some points because you're a really good dresser, well, congratulations. But don't worry too much about it. That's all I'm saying.

Your appearance is important. But it's not *that* important.

# 22. See the Reward

*"A picture is worth ..."*

Jackie was a friend of mine at Xerox and, man, did she love to travel. I would bet that she was in the Caribbean three or four times a year, and whenever she returned there were enough stories and pictures to keep us entertained until the next time she packed her bags.

Now, you might think that Jackie couldn't have taken her sales job very seriously. I mean, three or four Caribbean vacations seem like a lot of time away from her sales territory, right? But Jackie was a top performer at Xerox.

She won the prestigious President's Club award. She won Sales Rep of the Year. So it's not surprising, then, that Jackie was also an incredibly hard worker. There was no lollygagging around the office; no chit-chatting or just passing the time away. Nope. Jackie worked her butt off, and sold a lot of photocopiers in the process.

So how did she do it? How did she stay on top? What kept her motivated? How did she sell those copier machines day after day? And, of course, how did she manage to spend so much time on a beach in the Caribbean?

Well, part of the answer comes from the beach itself.

Recognition and reward mean a lot to salespeople. Some people sell for the money. Others sell for the prestige of being number one. Still others sell because they enjoy working with people, or they just love getting out there and mixing it up every day. In Jackie's case, I don't know what drove her to work so hard, or how exactly she managed to be so successful, but I do know that Jackie was very focused on one particular reward, and that reward was palm trees. She just loved to jump on that plane every two or three months and sit under those palm trees. And to remind herself, she would keep pictures and brochures of upcoming trips pinned up at her workstation. She would talk about those trips, stare at those palm trees, and remind herself that every customer complaint, every long day, every tough negotiation was all worth it. Very soon she would be back on the beach with a margarita in hand and that palm tree close by.

So, what motivates you? Do you want a new car? Maybe there's a new house in the works? Maybe you're hoping to tell your mom or dad that you were the number-one rep this year. Whatever the reward is, take a picture of it: the award, the car, the family project, the vacation spot, the new house—whatever it is that gets you moving and keeps you going. Put that picture in a place where you can see it each and every day. Your picture will remind you that your efforts are worth it. And maybe when you just don't feel like digging deep, and making that one last call…maybe that's the time when you will think to yourself, *"This could be the call that puts me on the beach."*

Look at your rewards, every day.

# Part  5

# Getting Prepared

# 23. "Winging It" Just Doesn't Cut It

*"I don't like to plan my sales calls...I keep them spontaneous...I have better conversations with my customers that way."*

What chance do you think we would have had of winning World War Two if the Allies had decided to let their armed forces "wing it"?

*Whatever feels good, boys—just use your intuition!*

Well, of course, after those generals were put out to pasture, somebody would have had to sit down and prepare an approach. They would have had to create a strategy, a plan of attack. (See Chapter 35, "Leverage Your Strengths.")

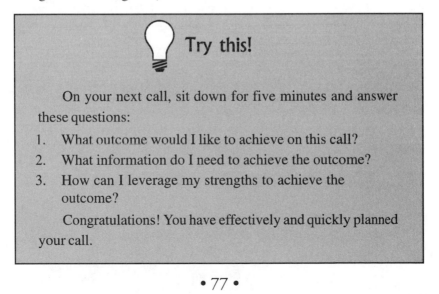

**Try this!**

On your next call, sit down for five minutes and answer these questions:

1.   What outcome would I like to achieve on this call?
2.   What information do I need to achieve the outcome?
3.   How can I leverage my strengths to achieve the outcome?

Congratulations! You have effectively and quickly planned your call.

*Don't ever go see your account on intuition alone!* Chances are you will miss something that you shouldn't. More importantly, customers know when you're winging it. Your lack of preparation, lack of an agenda, lack of focused questions, and lack of action and direction will make them question the need to spend their valuable time with you.

Carve out a strategy for every call. Your clarity of thinking will be obvious to all.

## IN REVIEW

Failing to plan is planning to fail!

# 24. Make Call Planning Simple, Fast, and Effective with the "GOTTA KNOWS"

*"Damn, I totally forgot to ask who the decision-maker is!"*

I used to cringe when some pie-in-the-sky head-office planner would produce yet another call planning sheet for me to add to my customer call plans. As if the mountains of other paperwork weren't enough. The worst offenders would ask us to complete lengthy and all-encompassing questionnaires with our customers. What were they thinking? Did they imagine that our sales calls were like market research interviews? Did they think that our customers would enjoy, or even agree to, a question-and-answer session? Maybe they had just confused selling with interrogation (okay, maybe that's a little harsh!).

We never used them, of course. When you're in front of customers, the last thing you want to do is destroy a good conversation by referring to your fourteen pages of call planning questions, so that you could ask yet another stale question about their "current needs" or some other calculated term. However, the bad news was that by ignoring pre-call planning, we ended up "winging it," and that meant calls would end without the needed information or commitment from the customer.

If you have an important call or meeting, but don't have the time to fill out lengthy call planning forms, I would suggest using the "GOTTA KNOWS."

Here's the idea. Every call should advance the sale and customer relationship in some way. The GOTTA KNOWS is a simple and short bulleted list of the information that you need in order to move forward in the process. In lieu of the onerous call planning forms, the GOTTA KNOWS is a one-pager that can sit on your lap during a meeting as a constant reminder to keep you on track. Now, let me throw out a significant caution here. I am not suggesting that you grill your customers with the bullets on your list. The bullets are meant to help you keep an open conversation focused around information that you need to know. Here's an example of one that I used on a recent call:

GOTTA KNOWS

- *Decision-making process*
- *Strategic plan*
- *Where's the pain?*
- *View of outsourcing*
- *Why are you supporting us on this one?*
- *Implementation obstacles*
- *Competitive threats*
- *New vice-president's power in organization*
- *Next steps*

That was it. That short list was the only paperwork that I brought into the two-hour call with an important executive customer.

It is refreshing to watch other salespeople who believe in the GOTTA KNOWS. I joined one associate for an executive call and found that she had developed her own version of the list. In fact, she defined her call success—or failure—on the basis of how many items she could tick off her list. Sure enough, I watched intently as she conducted a meeting that simply sounded like an intelligent business conversation—not an interview or typical sales call. It was an engaging and active dialog, and I could tell that the executive was impressed by her thoughtful questions (posed from her GOTTA KNOWS). When the conversation got a little bit off track, she would simply glance down at her list and redirect the discussion back to her GOTTA KNOWS. I also noticed that she made little check marks beside each bullet that was discussed to her satisfaction.

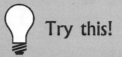 **Try this!**

Prior to your next call, ask yourself this question: What information do I need from this meeting in order to call it a success?

1. Pre-Call: On the assumption that you will be taking notes during your sales call, write a list of the items that you need—in point form—at the top of the page. You may want to think about the questions you will ask in order to extract the information in a meaningful way.

2. Call: This is the good part. The idea of the GOTTA KNOWS is to give you a question guide without its looking as if you're using a guide. Conduct the call as you would normally, but look at your list occasionally to ensure that the right questions are being asked and answered. Do not leave the call until your entire list has been satisfied.

3. Post-Call: Review the information that you have obtained. Record it in a way that will serve you in the future. Congratulate yourself on a job well done.

The end result: We got all of the information on the list and an action plan that advanced the sale. We did it with one short bulleted list as a guide. And we did it in a conversational style that built our credibility with the executive.

Very impressive.

*There is information about your customer that you have just got to know!*

## IN REVIEW

There is information about your customer that you need to know. If you want to get that information in the context of an intelligent business conversation, use your own version of the GOTTA KNOWS—a simple checklist of the critical information that you will need in order to advance the sale.

# 25. Smarter Is Better than Harder

*"Do you ever get the feeling that you're just beating your head against a wall?"*

I used to be impressed by people who worked long and hard hours. *"Wow, that's commitment—and commitment means success!"* But over time I noticed that some of those dedicated workers would continue to put in long and stressful days with only mediocre results to show for it. Unfortunately, when you don't produce the fruit from the labor, it doesn't take long before frustration sets in, and that is the case with many salespeople who work brutally long hours but never achieve their targets. You can actually see the stress etched in their faces as each long and unproductive day comes to a close. Sometimes I imagine the words behind their expressions:

*"What am I doing wrong? I'm working like a dog and I'm still missing quota. When is this going to get easier?"*

If that's what *you're* thinking, it won't get easier with effort alone (sigh)! The answer for me was to develop a "work smart and hard plan"—also known as a Time/Results Strategy. Sounds impressive, doesn't it? But it's not that difficult. A Time/Results Strategy is simply a work plan that looks at two things:

1.  your total available *time*; and
2.  the *results* that you need to achieve in that time.

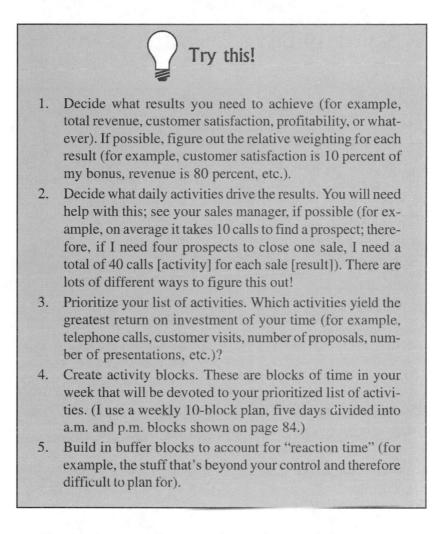

## Try this!

1. Decide what results you need to achieve (for example, total revenue, customer satisfaction, profitability, or whatever). If possible, figure out the relative weighting for each result (for example, customer satisfaction is 10 percent of my bonus, revenue is 80 percent, etc.).

2. Decide what daily activities drive the results. You will need help with this; see your sales manager, if possible (for example, on average it takes 10 calls to find a prospect; therefore, if I need four prospects to close one sale, I need a total of 40 calls [activity] for each sale [result]). There are lots of different ways to figure this out!

3. Prioritize your list of activities. Which activities yield the greatest return on investment of your time (for example, telephone calls, customer visits, number of proposals, number of presentations, etc.)?

4. Create activity blocks. These are blocks of time in your week that will be devoted to your prioritized list of activities. (I use a weekly 10-block plan, five days divided into a.m. and p.m. blocks shown on page 84.)

5. Build in buffer blocks to account for "reaction time" (for example, the stuff that's beyond your control and therefore difficult to plan for).

Use the *time* you have to get the *results* you need.

Here's the key. Once you have devised your strategy, *stick to it*. For example, if you have put aside one hour to look after customer issues, don't stop in the middle of your sales day to react to a minor customer issue (for example, their latest bill is inaccurate). You are not going to be able to fix it on the spot anyway, so put it off until your scheduled "issues hour." Now get back to that sales call you were planning. In the end, it will be far more important than the billing issue.

# A Sample 10-Block Time/Results Strategy

|  | Mon. | Tue. | Wed. | Thur. | Fri. |
|---|---|---|---|---|---|
| 8 - 8:30 | Day planning | | | | |
| 8:30 - 9:30 | Telephone calls, voice mail, e-mail & admin. | | | | |
| 9:30 - 11:30 a.m. block | Customer care calls Zone A/B/C | Prospecting & Visits Zone B | Prospecting & Visits Zone A | Buffer Time Zone A/B | Appt. Times Scheduling Zone C |
| 11:30 - 1 | LUNCH - Voice mail & customer follow-up (F/U) | | | | |
| 1 - 4 p.m. block | Prospecting & Visits Zone C | Appt. Times Scheduling Zone B | Appt. Times Scheduling Zone A | Appt. Times Scheduling Zone B | Buffer Time Zone A/C |
| 4 - 5 | Voice mail, e-mail, customer F/U & issue resolution | | | | |
| 5 - ... | Proposals & paperwork | | | | |

Zone A = downtown
Zone B = west
Zone C = central

Activity/Goals
Appointments scheduled: 10/week
Prospecting: 50/week

# In Review

Working hard isn't good enough—you have to work smart and hard.

# 26. Being Both "Hunter" and "Farmer" Is the Key to Constistency

*"If you don't like the roller coaster, get off the ride!"*

When I began selling, I thought that big commissions went to the best hunters—the elite class of salespeople. Hunters were a talented group of men and women charged with the difficult and treacherous job of flushing out new prospects and closing new business in a hotly competitive marketplace. And me? Well, I thought that I was a pretty darn good hunter in my own right, and business was generally good. But it wasn't long before I noticed the painful roller-coaster effect of the hunt. My sales life was characterized by up and down periods of high earnings (up) and little or no earnings (down) along the continuous cycle of finding and closing new business.

Fortunately, I had a few good mentors who taught me the meaning of the word "balance." While they were worthy adversaries in the hunting category, they had chosen to allot a considerable amount of time to farming. At first, I thought that they were just wasting a lot of good selling time.

*"Are they just babysitting their existing base of accounts because it feels good?"* I wondered. *"Or maybe they just want to avoid doing the really tough and important work of finding new clients."*

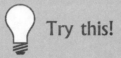 **Try this!**

The hunting/farming balance is a tough thing to control, because many of you will have no choice when it comes to how much you put into hunting and farming. But for those of you who do have control and a mix of accounts, I would suggest looking at your Time/Results Strategy and trying to create separate goals for your hunting and farming activities. Because your goals will drive the activities, think about a balanced set of activities that ensures that you are devoting at least some of your time to both hunting and farming, consistently every week.

Aside from strictly planning, I have found that farming is a good counterbalance to hunting. In other words, the next time you become discouraged by a painful or disappointing hunt, schedule in some time to visit a happy customer. While always a nice change of pace, these visits may open up some new doors in a place that is already well positioned to buy from you. If, on the other hand, you have been farming for a while and the experience is starting to get stale, take your success stories out on the hunt and try to find a new organization that could benefit in the same way that your farming accounts do.

No. Smart salespeople visit existing clients much as farmers tend their fields. They realize that it takes a lot less time and effort to "cultivate" an existing, profitable relationship than to go out and hunt for a new one.

Smart salespeople *balance* hunting and farming.

Good "farmers" schedule in specific times to visit their existing clients. During that time they build their contact base by exploring other areas of their customers' business. They also ensure that current business is meeting expectations. If expectations are being met, they are getting written or verbal references to use either somewhere else in the company or in another sales opportunity. If expectations are not being met, they are pulling in the right resources to fix the issues, to return another day. Ultimately, they are keeping their fingers on the pulse of the organization to ensure that when opportunity knocks, they'll be ready to answer.

And here's another thought. Unlike hunters, farmers don't have to search for prey. Farmers simply spot the best crops and tend to their health and growth continually. With a little attention and consideration, they can ensure that there will be cause to celebrate over the long winter months.

*Note*: There's an added bonus that comes from farming. It's a nice way to relieve the stress of getting rejected by strangers. If you're feeling a little down, go and see an account where you have been very successful building a relationship. If nothing else, basking in your own glory is a good way to drag yourself out of the dumps.

## IN REVIEW

Balancing your sales activities between hunting for new prospects and cultivating existing ones will help you achieve balanced results—results that will tend to even out the painful roller-coaster effect of opening and closing new accounts only.

# Part  6

# Going to
# the Right Place

# 27. Think Like Your Customers

*"That was another annoying salesman. I get at least three calls a day from someone trying to sell me a new phone system."*

One of the best-kept secrets in sales is the salesperson's ability to concentrate not on what is being sold, but rather on why a customer would want to buy. "Putting yourself in the shoes" of your customer will help you understand what their real problems are, and what your product or service will do to solve them. At the end of the day, if your proposal fills a big hole in your customer's sinking ship, there's a very good chance that you and your sale will go to the top of their priority list.

Let's start this "customer focus" idea by identifying your audience because different people will have different problems depending on their role in the organization. Different types of problems translate into different reasons for buying. Here are a few guidelines.

## OPERATIONS

If you are talking to operations (that's usually the bulk of employees in any organization), they are usually in react mode. For example, people on the floor in manufacturing react to a design specification; people in the billing department react to a sales order; people in customer service react to a call for service. Their "react" frame of reference means that *people who are in operations are worried about "fighting fires."* To think like these customers, you need to consider the fires they are dealing with, every day, and how you can help fight them.

# MANAGEMENT

If you are talking to management, don't worry so much about the fires. Managers are the checks and balances in an organization. It is their job to ensure that all is going according to plan, and therefore their issues are in the "here and now." They are concerned about *current performance relative to their goals and objectives*. If something is getting in the way of achieving their goals, they will not be happy. To think like these customers, you need to consider what's preventing managers from meeting their goals and objectives, and what you can do about it.

# EXECUTIVES

If you're talking to executives, never talk about product (sadly, sales reps do this because they love to talk about what they know—it's a very common mistake). Product features and benefits are almost always geared towards the firefighters, and therefore to operations people. Executives are not worried about fighting fires, because they have an army of people in their organization who are paid to fight them. *Executives are worried about what is on their horizon*. Their issues are connected to the future, and their success will be a measure of how well they "steer the ship." Things on their horizon include local and global economies, legislation, stock trends, information technology, market dynamics, emerging competitors, etc. To think like these customers, you need to consider where their ship is going and how your products or services can help them get there.

In summary, operations people are reacting, managers are checking and balancing, and executives are steering the ship. All three types of customers exist in every account. And it's up to you to position your products and services accordingly.

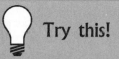 **Try this!**

Pick one of your largest accounts—one in which you have a good contact at all three levels—operations (firefighters), management (checks and balances), and executive (steering the ship).

1. Write down what you would like to sell this organization in the coming months (the product or service name, and total revenue).

2. List one person from each of the above three categories. Pick those whom you know well.

3. Beside each name, list the reason(s) why they would want to buy your product or service.

4. Review the list. Do the reasons fit their role in the organization? Are there any duplicate reasons among the contacts?

5. If the reason doesn't seem to match the role, or if duplications arise, might I pass a caution on to you? Watch out! Often, salespeople are guilty of assuming that they know the reasons, when really they are just guessing. For example, if you have listed similar reasons for distinctly different customers, I'm willing to bet that there are holes in your assumptions.

6. Try it again. If the duplications persist, it's time to make a sales call to uncover the real reasons why they would want to buy—or worse, the reasons they don't!

For example, suppose you are selling project management software to a large manufacturing organization. Your first meeting is with operations staff. They need to get better control of the project process because they frequently miss operational deadlines (reacting). You decide to discuss their need for coordination between departments. You discover that your project management software will help them work together with less confusion, hassle, and waste, so that deadlines are not missed.

Your second meeting is with management. You decide to discuss their recent initiatives to streamline the project process (checks and balances). You discover that your project management software will help their department reduce cycle time and improve their ability to accurately forecast budget, completion time frames, and resource requirements.

Your last meeting is with an executive. You decide to discuss the impact that time-to-market initiatives (like project management) have on the competitiveness of their organization (steering the ship). You discover that your project management software will reduce the time-to-market on new product initiatives by 10 percent, despite a recent downsizing. You also discover that your project management software will improve communication and coordination between departments, which means that the organization will respond more readily to major product modifications that are planned for next year.

Good job! You took the same project management software and gave different people different reasons to buy it.

Remember, customers buy for their reasons…not yours!

## IN REVIEW

Different types of customers care about different things. It's your job to position products or services according to how they will help different customer roles within the same account.

# 28. Hey You "Solution Sellers"— Call High and Wide

*"It's such a huge account. Who do you think makes the decision here?"*

Figuring out who you should approach in your accounts can be tricky business. Frankly, I don't think it matters who's first, as long as it doesn't stop there.

The secret to success lies in a multiple-contact strategy, especially in large, complex accounts, where lots of people have a say in who buys what, and from whom. In these cases, it is wise to adopt a "high and wide" call strategy.

## WHY CALL HIGH

"High" refers to executive-level, or senior staff, and you need to be calling here for three reasons.

First, higher levels of management typically make the decisions— enough said about that. (Warning: Don't underestimate the front-line or "shop floor" staff. These days they are held accountable for some pretty major decisions.) When looking for the right executive, I would suggest that the power base has shifted from corporate head office to field operations; in other words, the executives who are more in touch with customers often have more power, money, and influence than those at the corporate head office.

Second, if your solution(s) affect the entire company or at least more than one department (that is, "enterprise solutions"), or if your solutions are more strategic, integrated, or just plain old expensive, you will probably need the support of someone higher up the food chain. That's because you will need to deal with someone who can see the big picture, and has the power to influence that picture. Big-picture people tend to be removed from day-to-day operations (or "the trenches"), and therefore you will have to be calling high.

Third, executives can grant you access to the rest of the organization. Large or complex solutions have a high degree of risk. Front-line employees are often shy of salespeople who want to introduce yet more change and risk into their already chaotic lives. However, if you get the "okay" or "corporate blessing" to explore the organization, you will find that access to the trenches is much easier. Do yourself a favor. Become "knighted" by an executive so that you can more easily pass through their kingdom.

In summary, as a rule of thumb, always call high! If you are directed to a lower stratum of management, well, at least you tried. The good news is that if you make a good impression at the higher level, you get knighted. Best-case scenario: Calling high gets you to the decision-maker right away, and that's where the buck stops (thanks Harry).

*Note:* Beware of other sales reps who tell you *not* to call high. In my experience they just don't know how to do it (they go in and talk about products … arghhh) or they just don't have the guts. Anyway, if you are new to the account, you have nothing to lose. If an executive frowns at you, just plead ignorance. Being new to an account is a rare opportunity to establish relationships at a high level where decisions get made.

Also, a final note for those who think "I can't sell to an executive." Don't blow your chances for success because of your own fear of making a call on an executive. If you don't want to do it, find someone who will. Find an executive in your own organization with a "like ranking" and set up an executive exchange or breakfast meeting, or a golf game, if you like. Whatever it takes, don't let the opportunity of an executive relationship slip by.

# Why call wide

"Wide" refers to "across" the organization. Most organizations these days have decentralized their decision-making to some extent. Not long ago, centralization was the way to go. Decisions were made at the corporate head office, so many sellers would focus their efforts there. But over time, many corporations have come to realize that centralized decision-making is counterproductive because decisions are being made too far from the action. So, many big head-office locations and functions have been slimmed down or eliminated altogether. The valuable work that head office was doing still needs to be done, so much of it (along with the budget) has migrated to the "field" (where the customers are), because decisions can be made faster and by people who are more in tune with the marketplace and their customers.

A good way to figure out this centralized/decentralized thing is to ask your contacts for an organization chart. Even a quick glance should tell you something about how decisions are made. The pyramid structure will reinforce the old centralized paradigm, as decisions have to go up to the top for final approval. But today, don't be surprised to see organizational charts that look very confusing and complex as the pyramids are replaced by smaller operating groups with names like "customer business units" or "lines of business." Each has a reporting requirement to the head office, but each has its own operating managers or vice-presidents. When you see organization charts that have bundles or groups as opposed to the typical hierarchy, it's likely that decentralized decision-making has been embraced.

Outside of organizational structure, it's pretty much a given that people at the front of the action or on the shop floor have much more influence and decision-making capability than they used to.

What that all means to you is that decision-making doesn't happen in just one spot. You have to get out in the field and visit the different divisions and units. You also have to stay in touch with the traditional head-office folks, because they still have power and influence. In fact, when it comes right down to it—*you have to get to know the entire*

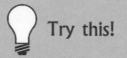 **Try this!**

Draw a simple schematic of a company that is a prospect for one of your solution sales (a sales cycle that has just begun—that is, the customer is "evaluating problems"). Your drawing should show the areas, divisions, locations, and departments of the customer's organization that your solution will "touch" and that may have some influence on the decision to buy.

With this visual aid completed, first decide who can make the decision here—who can say yes to a solution that touches all the areas you have drawn. Second, decide who and where you should be calling inside this drawing; more importantly decide, out of all of the potential names, titles, and places, who would be the most likely to support you, your company, and your proposal.

When you have completed the process, you should have a good indication of how high and wide you need to be calling to get the needed support for your solution sale.

*organization* to some extent. Don't let yourself get down to "deal time" and find that you have forgotten a powerful person who just happens to favor your competition.

Improve your chances for success by calling high and wide.

## In review

If you're selling a solution that affects an entire organization, then you will want to call high enough to get the decision, and wide enough to get the support for that decision.

# 29. There Are Only Two Types of Customers to Worry About

*"There are 1,500 people in their operation—that's a lot of people who have something to gain or lose from our solution. Who would you suggest we call on first?"*

We all know that there's always that one person at the end of the day who can make the decision to buy from you. We often call that person a decision-maker. However, we tend to be less aware of all the people who can influence the decision to buy from you. I like to think of these people as decision "catalysts." Remember your high school chemistry experiments? When you added the catalyst to a concoction of seemingly inert materials, there was always an interesting effect—an interaction with the other chemicals. You could always count on something spectacular happening, and I can remember taking a few steps back from the counter to avoid getting caught by whatever the "something" was. A decision "catalyst" also has an effect—an effect on your sale. Some catalysts are positive, and others are negative.

Positive catalysts are in your favor because they have something to gain from your proposal. Thus, they help you to advance the sale. Positive catalysts are good to have around. Negative catalysts are against you—they prefer your competitor, or they don't want to spend their money, or they just don't want to change, and therefore will block you on the premise "if it ain't broke don't fix it!" Negative catalysts have something to lose from your proposal, and therefore they will try to stop you from advancing the sale. With this idea in hand, here's a fun (albeit scary) little test that you can do with any of your larger accounts.

- Part 1: Identify your decision-maker by asking yourself this question: "Who can say yes to my proposal [where 'yes' is the authority to buy]?"
- Part 2: Now here's the tough part: Identify *every* person (or "title" if you don't know the name) who has the power to influence decision-making. Ask yourself this question: "Who are the catalysts? Who will have an effect—positive or negative—on the outcome of this sale?"
- Part 3: Looking at your list of people (one *maker* and lots of *catalysts*), put a check mark beside those whom you have contacted and who are in your favor. For the remainder of the list—that is, the people you have not contacted and/or who are not in your favor—you have an important question to answer: "With the time I have available, who on this list should I be calling? Who on this list do I need in my camp?"
- Part 4: With your list in hand, what actions will you take? What will you do to *engage* the positive catalysts—to help you advance the sale? And what will you do to *neutralize* the negative catalysts—to stop them from stopping you?

Don't ignore decision "catalysts." They will have an effect—positive or negative—on the outcome of your sale.

# Part 7

Opening the Door

# 30. Your Reputation Counts

*"Who are your customers in the health-care industry?"*

If you're selling a product that's worth five dollars, do you think that the reputation of your company is of great importance? I mean, how much of a reputation do you need to sell somebody a bag of potatoes or a box of envelopes? I don't know about you, but I buy all kinds of items in the five-dollars-or-less category, and I haven't got a clue who manufactures them (except that they come mostly from somewhere in Taiwan or China).

Why don't we care? Well, let's say that you're selling a pair of socks to me and the price tag is five dollars. What's my risk here? If I take them home and they fall apart in one wearing, what's the big deal? The worst-case scenario is I've lost a little bit of money. At this level, I don't care who the salesperson is or who they work for.

But then there's you, a professional salesperson. You will probably be representing a product or service with a price tag well beyond five dollars. Moreover, you may be selling solutions that are technically complex, that may affect many different people, processes, and departments in your customer's organization, and that could be a great asset to your customer's business if the solution is successful, or a major impediment if things go wrong. All of those factors—cost, complexity, interdependence, and impact—add up to *risk*—that is, your customer's risk of purchase.

When faced with risk of this nature, customers will always look at the vendor's reputation (that's you) as a measure of whether the risk is acceptable. Good reputation = lower risk. Bad reputation = higher risk. It's that simple. It should come as no surprise, then, that most customers will think through the following questions at some point in your selling cycle:

- Who are you? (Do I know you? Have we done business with you before?)
- How long have you been around?
- Who does business with you?
- Why do they do business with you?

If you happen to work for a reputable company, you may not have to answer those questions directly. But don't kid yourself; those questions are still being asked by your customers. And here's one really good reason why: If for some reason you fail—that is, your solution doesn't work—someone in your customer's organization is going to be very annoyed, and they will seek out *and* find the person who made the decision to buy from you. When they find the decision-maker—your customer—do you know what they're going to ask them?

- Who was the vendor? (Did we know them? Have we done business with them before?)
- How long have they been around?
- Who else does business with them?
- Why did those companies choose this solution?

There's an old expression that sums up the point of this chapter nicely. It comes from a time when International Business Machines (IBM) ruled the computer marketplace. Those were the days of the mainframe. Those were the days before the personal computer, Microsoft, and Bill Gates. IBM was by far the leader, and everybody knew it. So those clever IBM sales reps would not let that strength go unnoticed, particularly if their customer was thinking of considering a

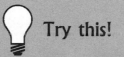 **Try this!**

Here's a reputation-building exercise that can help you open a new door.

1. Identify an industry in which you have a strong reputation.
2. Identify a prospective client in the same industry—one that you will be calling on to explore new sales opportunities.
3. Identify an existing customer (same industry) and outline the reasons they bought from you.
4. Script an opening call to your prospective client, citing examples of benefits from your existing customer. For example: "Hello, Ted. My name is John Smith. The reason I am calling you is because we have had a lot of success in your industry recently. At Company X we provided the following benefits....I would like to get some time on your calendar and discuss how we could get the same results at your organization."

smaller and lesser-known competitor's product. As the customer considered the risks—as all customers do—their IBM sales reps would whisper in their ear, "Remember, no one ever got fired for buying IBM."

You have two ways of addressing this issue with your customers:

1. If you're the one with the great reputation, remind your customers about it. Often.
2. If you're not the one with the great reputation, or, worst case, you are selling against the competitor who is well known as the biggest and/or the best, make sure that you sell the customer on yourself and your company, just as you would sell them on your product. Do not avoid the discussion. That's the kiss of death. Remember, your reputation will be considered in every major sale that you will ever make. So avoiding the question means that you are letting the customer make their own assumptions or, worse yet, letting your competition convince them that your reputation isn't good enough. Don't do that. Talk about your

great reputation. Give them examples of your customers in their industry. Explain why you have such a great and growing market share.

## IN REVIEW

Sell your company as you would your product because your reputation always matters.

# 31. Reference Selling Is Hard to Beat

*"The reason for my call is that one of your customers, Brad Thompson, thought that you would be a really good candidate for our products..."*

So you're in the middle of an important project and I call you on the telephone. Here's the bad news—I'm a salesperson. How soon can you get rid of me? You don't know me, you don't know my product, and you don't know my company. Goodbye.

The phone rings again. Oh no, another salesperson. How soon can you get rid of me? You don't know me, you don't know my product, and you don't know my company. *But* you do know Brad Thompson—he's one of your customers and a significant force in the industry. I also know Brad Thompson, and he thinks pretty highly of me, my product, and my company.

My guess is that you're willing to talk to me. Am I right?

'Nuff said.

Every time you make a sale, you need to follow up with a reference request. Go back to your customer and ask them to point you to someone new. But don't do it right away. Give the customer a chance to work the bugs out, or at least get used to the benefits of your solution. But when that time has come, make the call. Ask, "Jeff, now that your solution is up and running, I could use your help. Can you think of one or two contacts that could benefit from our product or service? Someone you know who could relate to our solution?" Always ask a satisfied customer for a reference. It's the most powerful prospecting tool you can use.

# 32. Get Your Foot in the Door with a WIIFM

*"I'm just stepping into a meeting right now—what is it you want?"*

Picture this: You're in your pajamas. You are enjoying a good video or a *Seinfeld* rerun after a long hard day at work. A smile comes to your face as your thoughts drift to a well-deserved stress-free evening. Without warning, your happiness is shattered by the doorbell. Annoyed, you get up and walk to the door. *"Who could it be at this hour?"* Well, guess what? It's a stranger and, worse yet, a salesperson! My question to you is this: *What would that salesperson have to say to convince you to stop what you're doing and listen?* It would have to be something pretty darn interesting, wouldn't it?

The clever sales rep at your front door will be prepared to deliver a WIIFM ("What's in It for Me?"). A WIIFM is a brief but clear statement of what *the listener* stands to gain by listening to what you have to say.

Remember WIIFMs as you prepare to make a prospecting call (or when getting ready for an important meeting or telephone conversation). The people with whom you wish to speak may not be watching a video in their pajamas, but they have plenty of other distractions to keep them busy. Each of their distractions competes with you and your message!

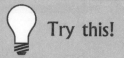 Try this!

Here's a simple test for you. Before you make your next big prospecting call (say, a call to "get your foot in the door" with an important executive), jot down the answers to these questions:

- What does this executive do to earn a big paycheck every month?
- What obstacles are (or could be) getting in the way of what he/she does?
- What value can I bring to the table? How can I make this executive more successful with my products or services?

Now it's time to write down your discovery in the form of an opening statement, and be sure to include something like "The reason I am calling is … [insert WIIFM]."

PS: After ten years of selling, I still write down my opening statements. It may sound simplistic, but I have found that it still helps me sound crisp and clear, while reducing my stress (it can be scary calling senior executives).

So, before you make the call, think about how your customer will personally benefit. Answer the question: *Why would this customer want to listen to me?*

Let me give you an example of how a WIIFM might sound. You are making a prospecting sales call based on your new "contact management software" product. Below are three examples of how you might approach a certain customer who is the manager of a new call center that is having some difficulty managing its expanding operation. The first two approaches do *not* focus on the customer. Compare them with the last example, and then draw your own conclusions.

1. A reason that relates to your product: "The reason I'm calling is to tell you about our new contact management software that automates outbound calling processes, and manages existing client databases."

2. A reason that relates to you: "The reason I'm calling is that I happen to be in your area tomorrow and I wanted to take the opportunity to drop by and tell you about our new contact management software."

3. A reason that relates to your customer (a WIIFM): "The reason I'm calling is to get some time on your calendar, so that I can show you how to effectively manage the rapid growth in your operation, eliminating the frustration and time-wasting that you're experiencing now."

If you were the call center manager at the other end of the phone, which approach would have sparked your interest enough to carry on the conversation or set an appointment?

Give your clients a good reason to see you—use a WIIFM!

## IN REVIEW

Customers are busy people, which means they need a reason to see you—there has to be something in-it-for-them!

# 33. Your Customers Are Waiting for a Special Phone Call

*"If I could just hire someone to get through my e-mail and answer the phone, I might actually get some work done around here!"*

Consider the life of today's decision-makers. Imagine that they are sitting at their desks, working feverishly, racing against the clock. There's no doubt in my mind that the vast majority of "worker bees" out there have that exact same mindset: "Four hours of work to finish in ten minutes." It's about lots of stress, lots of change, and lots of uncertainty. Frankly, some days are less about accomplishment and more about survival.

Anyway, let's say that you are that decision-maker, and you are sitting at your desk in the midst of this mayhem when the phone rings. Uh-oh—no doubt this is another pesky sales rep trying to push a product or service down your throat. It's the last thing you need right now.

You answer the phone reluctantly, but a smile comes to your face. This is not a sales rep—or at least not the type of rep that you're used to hearing from. This person has been thinking about *your* business. He's talking about issues that concern you. What's this? He's been thinking specifically about an article that was written about you in yesterday's newspaper, an article that points out how successful your competition has become at winning market share. No kidding? He has worked with other companies like yours and he knows how to improve one area of your life that needs improving. *"Yes, 2:00 p.m. would be fine. I look forward to meeting you."*

You hang up the phone, pleasantly surprised, but feeling a little bit puzzled. *"Wait a minute, he didn't say what he was selling. Well, I guess I'll find out next Thursday."*

Makes you think, doesn't it?

# Part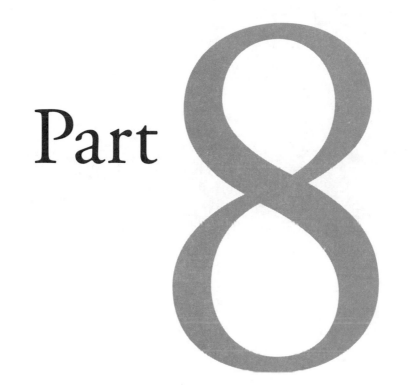

## Discovering and Developing

# 34. Find the Fires

*"So why do you think they'll buy from us?"*

Here's a simple thought. The likelihood of your selling a glass of water to me is directly proportional to my degree of thirst.

In a large or complex sale, there are people out there who don't care that your product can leap tall buildings in a single bound. That's probably because your product or service, while interesting and effective, does not have any bearing on one of their "fires." Think of sales that have been stalled for long periods of time. Think of proposals that are collecting dust in a distant file cabinet. Think of customers who seem to look at ten thousand competitors only to decide that their current system "will do for now." Think about customers who will not budge from their lowball offer.

Why does that happen? Because in every one of those examples *the customer could live without your product or service. He just wasn't that "thirsty"!*

So here's the big pearl of wisdom. Decision-makers are often out of the action. Yes, there are major fires burning all around them, all of which are well documented in your proposal. But frankly, to the decision-maker, the fires are someone else's problem (someone lower in the hierarchy) and, consequently, each blaze seems like just a small blip

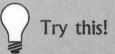

## Try this!

Go back to your account list—the list that documents all of your current opportunities. Try and identify, by name, the customers who are getting burned in those accounts—burned by fires that you can fix. If you come across a company for which no such name exists, make a note in your day planner to call on them. (You are at a significant disadvantage if there is no one in your customer's location who is getting burned because you may not be giving them a compelling reason to buy.)

Once you have identified the new contact by name, go and make a call to discuss the fire in greater detail. If this new contact believes that you have something to help put the fire out, you may have found a strong catalyst in your bid to make this sale a reality.

on their radar screen. (See Chapter 27, "Think Like Your Customer.") They have other, bigger issues to deal with.

The solution is this. There is always one person in the organization who is getting burned really badly. One person who takes the brunt of the responsibility for the fire. One person who is motivated to put the fire out because his/her life will be vastly improved as a result. And most of all, this one person has the power of influence: a *decision catalyst*!

Find such persons. Coddle them. Love them. Buy them coffee. Talk to them. Listen to them. Know their operations inside and out.

*Sell them!*

These are the people who will hound your decision-makers to make the change. And if you could find one person in every account that fits this description, and if you could sell this person on you and your fire fixer, you would be the most successful sales representative of all time.

## IN REVIEW

Find the customers who are getting burned by problems that you can fix! If they are getting burned badly, chances are they will help you make the sale if you can position your fire fixer properly.

# 35. Leverage Your Strengths

*"I have no idea why they bought from us in the past—who cares?"*

I used to avoid the whole notion of "strategy." It seemed to me that strategic thinking was this mysterious academic discipline that only reared its head at monthly sales meetings or product kickoffs. I figured I was the "doer" and not the "thinker," and so it would be best to let the "suits" upstairs worry about sales strategy.

But then I learned an interesting thing about military strategy that I think every salesperson can benefit from. General MacArthur in World War II obviously didn't just play his battles by ear; he had to devise a strategy. He had to come up with a plan for the Allies' advance on the Japanese. Now, I'm sure that it would be a complex and dizzying process to analyze the genius of his strategy, but the fundamentals of MacArthur's approach are similar to those of a sales rep approaching a sale. It all boils down to strengths and weaknesses. According to the book *Strategic Selling* by Miller Heiman, *a strategy is simply a plan that leverages your strengths and overcomes your weaknesses.*

Give it a whirl. Pick an account that you are working on right now. *Where are your strengths in that account?* Do you have a strong advocate inside the customer's organization? Do you have a perfect solution "fit"? Do you have a good reference? Do you have a good account history? Perhaps you've just done an outstanding job at

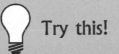

## Try this!

Pick one of your current sales situations that is sitting in the doldrums. In other words, it's still a good prospect but it doesn't seem to be going anywhere, and your efforts to move the sale forward have failed. Do a little thinking on this account. Chances are, you have a few weaknesses that may prove to be your undoing, but forget about them for now. Think about your strengths. What is it about your product, service, relationship, image, history, etc. that are strong advantages for you?

Now here's the thing. Use them! Deploy your strengths! Create an action plan that leverages one of your strengths to move the sale forward (read this chapter over again if you are having a hard time coming up with ideas). Sales that have stalled do not revive themselves on their own. Revitalize the opportunity. Leverage a strength!

servicing this account over time. Whatever those strengths may be, we typically don't do anything with them, because we often spend the bulk of our time worrying about our weaknesses.

We are looking for unique ways to beat a strong competitor, or we're trying to minimize a price objection, or we're trying to reassure the customer that the blip in customer service last month will never happen again. Meanwhile, our strengths—the really good stuff that got us there in the first place—have taken a back seat.

Get out there and leverage your strengths! Ask your strong customer advocate to make a call to support your proposal. Make a special trip to outline the reasons "why" you have the perfect solution fit and the positive repercussions that will come of it. Write a reference letter that highlights the business results achieved through your solution at another company. Write a letter documenting your excellent relationship over the years and the value that relationship brings to the table. Bring a representative from service into your account to illustrate the business impact of reliable service—a service that your customer cannot live without.

Don't let your strengths go unused. Leverage them.

## IN REVIEW

As sellers, we tend to dwell on our weaknesses at the expense of our strengths. Take your strengths out of the closet and put them squarely in your customers' line of sight.

## RECOMMENDED READING

Miller Heiman, Inc. does a good job in the strategy arena. I recommend their book *Strategic Selling*®, which gives the reader a solid grounding in strategic selling principles.

# 36. A Problem Is Only a Problem When the Customer Thinks It's a Problem

*"It was a good proposal, but I think we'll hold off until next year. Thank you very much for all of your time and effort!"*
—A variation on the "perception is reality" theme

I can remember getting very excited about a customer that was using an old beat-up photocopier. I made a visit to check on it and discovered that the copies were so bad that just reading the copies was becoming a challenge.

I was counting my commission dollars with every smeared copy that belched from the old beast. I thought this was going to be an easy sale. (*I can't believe this "boat anchor" is still here. How did the last sales rep miss it?*) Well, the last rep didn't miss it. He had drooled just as I had, and like me, he had put together a very elaborate proposal that made the upgrade to a new, high-quality copier almost a "no-brainer."

The two proposals, the previous rep's and my own, wound up side by side in the client's very fat "Photocopier" file, accompanied by the seven nearly identical versions from the many reps who had come calling over the past two years. "No sale!" When I saw that file, I felt like a goat, but I learned an important lesson. While my proposal addressed problems that I had discovered, *it never occurred to me that my problems were not necessarily the customer's problems.*

In this case, image quality was not an issue in the eyes of the customer. Now you might be thinking the same thing I was, when the customer said, "No thanks": "Is this guy crazy? These photocopies are almost unreadable."

But in the customer's eyes, the problem of poor quality was a minor inconvenience. He had another machine down the hall for use when high quality was needed, and this old clunker never really gave him that much trouble. So what if it smeared the pages? He only needed to use it for the occasional internal copy, so to him image quality just wasn't a big deal.

Herein lies the lesson. If you think you have identified the problem of the century, the problem in your customer's office that your solution will fix, the problem that will reap huge rewards for your customer, bring in huge revenue, and make you look like a hero—a word to the wise: Make sure your customer shares your perception. Ask the question: *"I noticed that the image quality is poor. Is that a concern of yours?"*

If the answer is no, then by all means try to change the customer's perception, but don't waste precious time writing proposals for problems that your customers don't care about.

## RECOMMENDED READING

Neil Rackham does an excellent job reviewing "problems" and customer perceptions in his book *Spin Selling*. It's a must-read for all corporate sellers.

# 37. Don't Be Afraid to Change Your Customer's Comfort Zone

*"We're in good shape. I certainly don't see any major changes on the horizon."*

People like to stay in their comfort zone. It's human nature. The more things change, the more inclined people are to hold on tight to the few remaining things that don't change. Unfortunately, depending on just how deeply rooted your customers are, their zone can be a major impediment to sales. While you see the solution of the century, your customer sees danger in their zone.

First things first. It's your job to change the world's comfort zones, because the people who are in them are often not motivated to do it themselves. In truth, when you make a successful change to your customer's zone, they owe you a debt of gratitude, because too much comfort leads to complacency, and too much complacency leads to the unemployment line. This is a big deal, because as salespeople, remember, we are the agents of change. In other words, every sale becomes a risk and a departure from your customer's zone. There's no getting around it!

Put another way, it's your job to confront your customer's comfort zone and make it *uncomfortable*! And there are two ways to do it:

1. Convince them that their comfort zone is more of a threat to their business than the change you are proposing.

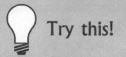

## Try this!

When you get the opportunity, ask one of your bigger customers to recall a time when they were operating outside their comfort zone (that is, not enough staff, not enough budget, too much change, etc.). Ask them to describe the situation: what was happening in their corner of the world, how were they feeling, and what they did about it. With the answers to those questions in mind, ask your customer one more thing: "What could I be doing to improve or change your comfort zone?" (You should get an interesting answer to that one!)

For example, while their current voice mail system is working just fine, show proof that their growth will outstrip capacity and result in some very big cracks in their comfort zone. While changes to a new system would be disruptive, they would pale in comparison to the chaos of the voicemail disaster just waiting to happen.

2. Convince them that you are, in fact, extending their comfort zone with the change you are proposing.

For example, while the current voice mail system is working just fine, show proof of how upgrades to the memory and security will improve the system and decrease the likelihood of a disaster down the road.

## IN REVIEW

As salespeople, it's our job to change the world's comfort zones. The problem is that people, by nature, resist change. Success hinges on our ability to adjust our customers' comfort zone in one of two ways: Convince them that their comfort zone is actually more of a risk than the course of action we are proposing, or convince them that we are in fact extending their comfort zone with the change that we are proposing.

# 38. Anticipating a Need Is Far Better than Responding to One

*"Your timing is uncanny. I was just thinking about giving you a call!"*

It's the difference between setting the pace for your competition and chasing after them. Which would you prefer?

*Get out there and get to know your customers!*

If you're the one developing a strong relationship with your customers, it will be *you* who finds the business issue, *you* who develops the need, and *you* who positions your company to win, long before any competitor's proposal is written.

When you have *that* advantage, competitors can only follow and react, or just get left out of the picture altogether.

It reminds me of an old saying:

There are those who make it happen …

those who watch it happen …

and those who wonder … "What just happened?"

*Find the need before it finds you, and you will win!*

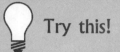

## Try this!

Think of a current customer who is favorably disposed to you and to your company, but who is not in the buying window at the present time. As far as they are concerned, everything is fine: "Don't call us, we'll call you!"

On a sheet of paper, write the name of the company and then draw two straight lines down the center of the page, dividing it into three equal columns.

In the left column, document this customer's business objectives for the year. Where are they trying to get to? (If you don't know, you may want to peruse the Internet or review their annual report.)

In the center column, for every business objective describe any obstacles that exist.

In the third column, for every obstacle come up with a product or service solution that will fix it.

Congratulations! You have just anticipated your customer's need. Now it's time to call them and ask for an appointment. If they are hesitant to grant you the time (remember, they are happy with the way things are), say, "I believe that I have found a way to overcome obstacle X in order to achieve business objective Y." Then make sure you have your pen handy to schedule in the appointment.

## In review

Anticipating your customer's needs gives you a jump-start on the competition. When you anticipate, your competitors are left to jump over a bar that you have set for them.

# 39. Your Nose Is a Powerful Sales Tool

*"Did you notice the lineups at the photocopier? Remind me to call the Director when we get back to the office."*

Ah, the nose! What a unique sensory object. Did you know that your olfactory sense (to smell, that is) is the most powerful sense associated with long-term memory? It's a scientific fact. Smells conjure up past places, people, and, of course, food!

The nose can also be used as a sales tool, but not in quite the same way. One of my greatest influences, my first Xerox sales manager, Steve, had a tremendous gift of the "nose," and fortunately he passed some of his skill along to me. I remember one day Steve and I were sitting in a customer's reception area. I was drifting aimlessly, waiting for our customer to greet us. This was a time I hated—sitting in reception, killing time. While deep in thought, I was oblivious to Steve, who was engaged in quite a different activity. Steve was sitting beside me, and while he looked suspiciously bored, as though he would fall asleep at any moment, he was in fact quite busy. *He was using his nose!*

In sales, the nose is a metaphor for the power of observation. Steve was watching, listening, and otherwise "taking it all in." He noticed that the reception area was in chaos, due in part to the switchboard's outdated technology. He listened to the phone conversations and noted the hint of desperation in the voice of the receptionist, who just couldn't handle the growing volume of calls. He looked around at the decor and noticed the attention to detail that signifies a firm's pride in its business. He even took the time to read a few of the achievements framed and posted on every wall. And he heard the many sounds coming from just beyond the entranceway—sounds of photocopiers he could identify by model number, despite the fact that they were hidden from view.

In little more than a coffee break our client arrived, and by that time Steve had answers to questions he would never have to ask. He had sniffed out some clues to the business and to opportunities we might pursue. We had a head start! We had Steve's nose!

*You've got a nose—use it!*

# Part 9

# Following Up

# 40. Get Customers "Live"

*"I left another message for Bill—that's the third one today."*

- E-mail ...
- Office voice mail ...
- Mobile voice mail ...
- Home voice mail ... (sigh)
- Home e-mail ...
- Paging ...
- A receptionist ...
- A co-worker ...
- Mail ...

Take your pick. How would you like to leave a message for your customer today? And when you've left your message, will you feel as if you've accomplished something?

Thanks to the joys of modern technology, we are overwhelmed by messages. *Please reply. Very Important. For Your Information.* I don't know about you, but I don't like leaving messages for my customers, because I feel like just another voice in a sea of voices—another request in an ocean of requests ...

There is an amazing alternative. It's called "direct communication." What a concept! Do yourself a favor the next time you get a voice mail message: Push the "0" button and talk to a live person. Find out where your customer can be reached, and when. Try to catch your customer at those times or during the off-hours—that is, before 8 a.m. or after 5 p.m.—when your mediocre competitors are sleeping.

The truth is, your customers will receive so many messages that they won't return many of them. It's not that they're discourteous. It's just that they don't have the time to reply to every single message, and since you're an outsider, and perhaps even someone they don't know, there's a good chance that your message will go to the bottom of their priority list. Sorry.

Here is the basic rule of thumb: *If there's a way to talk to your customer "live"—then do it.*

# 41. Don't Expect Anybody to Call You Back

*"I wouldn't waste your time. She never returns calls."*

Following up is to selling what breathing is to the front crawl. If you forget to do it, you're going to end up at the bottom of the pool.

There's something that you have to accept when you wander into this magical world of selling! *Customers often don't return calls.* But don't worry about that. It's not a customer's job to get hold of *you*. It's *your* job to get hold of the customer. Even though returning phone calls might seem like common courtesy, the truth is, if you start to expect customers to return your calls, you're in for some disappointment and frustration.

Allow me to explain. I was chatting with a customer service representative the other day, and she was telling me about the pain and aggravation that she suffered as a result of a customer that didn't respond to her voice mails. "Imagine, I've left two messages for the guy today, and he still hasn't returned my calls."

My initial thought was, "Why does that surprise you?" but I chose not to say anything because it occurred to me that her view of the world was very different from my own (and rightly so).

In her world, her message was related to a tangible thing, something that required a response. In this case, it was a confirmation of a training and installation date. That's pretty tangible. It's also important to the customer who will want to confirm the training and installation date, just as much as my customer service rep wants closure on the issue. The date is important to both parties. So my guess is that the customer will probably reply to the message, and that there is some logical explanation for the current delay.

But let's get you involved in this scenario. Let's suppose that your message was the next message in this customer's voice mail box (the message that follows our request for a training and installation date). Perhaps you've left a prospecting message or a request for references. Maybe you are calling to ask some questions about their operation, or to make an appointment, or perhaps you want to deliver a proposal. In each and every one of those cases, *you need the customer more than the customer needs you.* If the customer had message categories, I would guess that you would fall into the "if I get around to it" pile, while my customer service rep would go into the "get back to her by the end of day" pile. The fact is, I know many customers who have voice mail systems that fill up to capacity more than a few times during the average day. They will tell you bluntly that, when retrieving messages after a meeting, they will simply erase unimportant calls on the assumption that if the call is really that important, whoever made it will call back. That's not so good for the sales rep who is counting on a return call.

So what's my point here? Simple. My customer service rep, and many, many other types of workers and professionals out there, expect and deserve to hear back from customers. But we as salespeople are not like them. Learn to accept that. Whether you deserve it or not, don't expect the return call. Take the initiative, and follow up.

## SOME BASIC FOLLOW-UP RULES

1. Following up is your job.
2. Don't ask your customers to follow up with you—they very likely may not.
3. If the customer says, "I'll call you," suggest a contingency follow-up: "Great, Katherine, but if you get tied up I'll call you on Friday afternoon. Is that a good time for you?"

4.  Avoid leaving voice mails, especially if you're in the early stages of the sale (that is, when the customer doesn't know you that well).

5.  When leaving voice mail, keep your message short and stick to the point. Use your KISS and WIIFM skills here!

6.  If you do leave a voice mail or an e-mail, write a note to yourself to call back after a reasonable period of time.

# 42. E-Mail Can Be a Great Tool (But It Can Also Be a Colossal Waste of Time and Energy)

*"How could I have 35 new e-mails? All I did was go to the cafeteria to get a cup of coffee. Give me a break!"*

Here it is—your personal sales e-mail guide.

E-mail is like anything else. It's a great tool or a lousy tool, depending on who's at the wheel. And while it's still got a lot of sex appeal out there, thanks to the Internet, the bottom line is that e-mail is just another way to get a message to a customer. Your success with e-mail will be a measure of the quality and quantity of your message.

Consider your friends, family, and co-workers. Chances are, many or most of them have e-mail. And if you ask what irks them most about e-mail, I would guess it's got something to do with volume. There's just too much junk out there. And that sentiment correlates to my own feeling about mail of any kind. Paper mail. Voice mail. E-mail. Lots of people want to add to your pile of useless information. So, if you're planning on using e-mail as a sales tool, avoid being the "agent of junk." You're not doing yourself any favors. Read on.

E-mail is just mail. It's a message, plain and simple. But for a sales rep, it can be much more than just mail. Let's consider the advantages:

1. It's instantaneous. For all intents and purposes, the moment you send an e-mail is roughly the same moment it lands in your customer's in-basket. That means you can reach cus-

tomers quickly, providing that they have their e-mail programs running and they check their e-mail frequently.

2.  You don't get screened. Thanks to the wonders of cyberspace, it's safe to say that e-mail is usually getting right to the person on the address. For the most part, nobody is standing in the way to block you. (Watch out for executives; often they have someone screening their e-mails.)

3.  It's a written record. Because e-mails can be easily archived, you can go back to them when you need to verify things that were said, or things that weren't said.

4.  It can help your customers think of you. You can easily customize each e-mail with your name, address, logo, web site, etc., so that sooner or later your customers will begin to recognize you and your interest in their business.

5.  You don't have to worry about flubbing it. I can't tell you how many times I must have sounded like a "doofus" because my voice mail was choppy or distracted, or just plain stupid (by the by, these days you can review your voice mails before sending them, usually by pressing "*" or "#" after you have left your message). But with e-mail, thanks to your friendly neighborhood keyboard, you can delete any confusing word or phrase and type in what you really mean to say. Every e-mail can be a literary work of art. And if you have to send the same message to lots of different people, the magic of cut-and-paste is a beautiful thing. Be sure to proofread your message before you send it. Proper grammar and correct spelling *do* make a difference.

The trick to e-mail is the same as the trick to voice mail. Both are messages that have a very short window of time during which the customer tunes in or, conversely, tunes you and your message out. And since our customers are generally getting more and more e-mail these days, that means the "window of opportunity" is getting smaller and smaller. The problem is magnified further if your customer doesn't know you. A quick look at your address will tell your customer if you are a familiar face. If they don't recognize your name, then it's imperative that your message get their attention.

On that note, the essence of this chapter is brought to light: *Effective e-mails are e-mails that sell.* Your e-mail must engage your customer and commit that customer to reading it and then acting on it. It's no different from selling people over the phone or face to face. Wait a minute—it is different. It's tougher because e-mail is much easier to delete.

Here are a few guidelines to help you avoid the "deleted items" outcome.

1. Make the subject compelling. If you want to sell toothbrushes, don't type "Toothbrushes" in the subject field. Make it something that everyone will want to read. My guess is that "Improving Your Smile" will get more people to open the message than "Toothbrushes for Sale."

2. Make it short and sweet. Time is of the essence. Every day I get more e-mails, but the last time I checked, there were still 24 hours in the day. Something's gotta give. So the more messages your customers receive, the less time they have to devote to any one message. Make their lives easy. Give them a concise message.

3. Relate your message to the customer's business. Resist the urge to write volumes about you, your company, or your product. Get right to the point. What's in it for them? (Sound familiar?)

4. Include a "purpose" and a "next step." The former will keep them reading, and the latter will get you the action that you need to move the sale forward.

## THE E-MAIL WARNING LABEL

Please note: E-mail is not a substitute for sales. It's just another tool in your kit bag. Too much time behind your laptop or monitor means too much time spent away from your customers—time that could have been spent building relationships. E-mails don't sell, but they can help you to sell.

I would like to conclude this chapter with a sample. I would also like to suggest that you go back and read a few of your old e-mails. Or write a couple of sample e-mails, and then read them back while imagining that you're the customer. Is your message compelling? Short and sweet? Related to the customer's business? Complete with a purpose and next step?

## SAMPLE E-MAIL

**To:**     ted@excellentadventure.com

**From:**   buffy@vampire.com

**Subject:**  Great Results from E-commerce Meeting. Need Your Involvement

The purpose of this e-mail is to summarize our success at the e-comm meeting and confirm your attendance at our next meeting this Tuesday, July 10th, at 10:00 a.m.

As you know, Bill and I spent a few hours reviewing your e-commerce problem, namely your need for improved automation and control during file transfer. Ted believes the next step is a walk-through of our solution. We are planning on meeting at 10:00 a.m. next Tuesday at your office for an hour. During that time we will demonstrate how our software solution will solve your IT resource issue and reduce your support costs, all in the process of automating and controlling your e-commerce file transfer. Bill thought you would be very interested in our ability to reduce support costs, among other things.

Can you make it? If not, I would be happy to re-schedule. Please reply.

Thanks.

Buffy

# Part 10

# People

# 43. Everybody Wants to Win

*"This is all very interesting, but what's it going to do for me?"*

As we explored in the "What's in It for Me" chapter (Chapter 32), self-interest is an integral part of every human being who plans on surviving on this planet from one day to the next. Mother Nature is responsible for this "instinct," if you will, by programming all of her plants and animals to compete in a world of limited resources. As a member of the human species, it doesn't matter whether you're Attila the Hun or Mother Teresa—this is not about being good or bad. It's simply a function of the natural world that we live in. Everyone, by nature, *wants to win.*

So, what has this got to do with selling? Well, if every human being needs to win, and all of your customers are presumably human beings, then it would seem logical that all customers will be motivated, at least in part, by how your proposals make them winners.

Your task is to get to know your customers well, so that you can figure out how your product or service appeals to their need to win. The trick is, humans are peculiarly different in this regard, and given the same set of circumstances may win in completely different and some-times unusual ways. So figuring out how the individual "wins" isn't necessarily easy.

Here's an example:

Let's suppose you are a top pen salesperson. Your pen might appeal to three different "wins" of three different customers in the same organization:

- Customer 1 wants to feel important—that is his win. He wants a pen that stands apart from the others. Customer 1 will pay attention to the craftsmanship, quality, or prestige of the pen. Customer 1 wants to feel special and to be included in the company's elite class.

- Customer 2 is far more interested in the "price versus performance" ratio of the pen. She always looks for the balance between high quality and good pricing. More important, this pen purchase will be watched by Customer 2's boss. If the boss can be impressed by a wise purchase, there may be a promotion forthcoming for Customer 2, and that's definitely a big win.

- Customer 3 doesn't really care about pens at all. He is more interested in making everyone happy. Customer 3's win is based on peer group acceptance. He will support the pen purchase decision as long as everyone else does.

So many different personal agendas all for the sake of a simple pen. *So how do you figure out wins?*

Well, it isn't easy. Take company politics, for example. Now there's a subject that is all about wins, and I have found that most political people "keep their cards close to their chest." Can you imagine a sales rep asking: "Tell me, are you well liked by your employees?" or "Is it true you are trying to get your boss fired?" Chances are you are not going to ask those questions any more than a customer would be willing to answer them. *Wins are personal and consequently are often well guarded. (Strategic Selling®–Miller Heiman).*

There are two messages here:

1. Get to know your customers. If you are well known to your customers, and trusted by them, they will tend to let their guard down, revealing clues about how you can make them win.

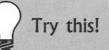

## Try this!

Pick an account that is not in good shape, one that is aligned with the competition and is offering no signs of encouragement to you. Identify the main character, or your nemesis, if you will. That is, the customer contact who is making sure that you stay out of the account—or, at least, is making sure that the current competitor stays in.

Now comes the tough part. Try to step back from the situation and analyze this customer at a personal level. Why does he or she want you out, or the competition in? What, personally, does this person stand to lose or gain?

If you don't know, or you feel that your answer is at best speculation and at worst a guess, develop a plan to find out. Who knows this person in his or her organization? Who knows this person in your organization? What information can you collect to help you determine his or her own unique wins? One thing is for sure, many seemingly hopeless sales have been turned around by a salesperson who was smart enough to tap into their customer's self-interest and find a way to make that person win.

2.  Never forget about wins. They are always there. People are human and, therefore, whether they want to admit it or not, at least part of their buying decisions are motivated by their self-interest. Your ability to identify that self-interest and position your product or service around it is a key factor in your success.

*Success is finding a way to make your customer win!*

## IN REVIEW

All customers are people, and all people want to win! It's instinct! Therefore, there is always the personal element in every sale, which can serve to help you or hurt you. The challenge is twofold. The first is understanding your customers well enough to determine their wins. The second is understanding how to position your solution so that these are satisfied. These two skills are extremely important and equally difficult.

## RECOMMENDED READING

Miller Heiman takes the concept of "wins" to another level. *Strategic Selling®* is a must-read if the subject of "wins" is appealing to you.

# 44. People Buy from People They Trust

*"I would say that my biggest strength is my ability to develop a strong relationship with my clients. I always do that first, before ever talking about my solution or my company. I figure if I can sell them on me, then everything else just follows."*

This selling truth ranks right up there among the top. But let's be careful about the wording. I've heard it said, "People buy from people they *like*." Close, but no cigar! There are volumes of business failures that could have been avoided had the company relied more on sound business judgment and less on personal ties.

Now don't get me wrong—it's great to be friends with your customers! In fact, a good rapport can really open up the lines of communication and establish trust. I'm just throwing out a significant caution: Don't rely on friendship as a mechanism to get the business. More than ever, today's customers face enormous risks when making buying decisions. Bottom line, there is just not enough time and money to take uncalculated risks in support of a friendship.

On the other hand, people are people. I don't care if you are selling soap dishes or submarines—there is a human being doing the selling and a human being doing the buying, and therefore the emotional element has a part to play in every sale.

*After all, people buy from people.*

Here's the happy medium, then. You don't have to be liked, but you do have to be trusted. People need to feel that after all is said and done, you—yes, you personally—are going to come through for them. It's true. You can't hide behind that big company name or reputation. As far as the customer's concerned, they are buying from you, and therefore it is your behavior and your actions that will establish trust.

I coached one high performer who really believed in this. He would spend a great deal of time with his accounts in an effort to establish personal trust. If there was a service problem, he was there to make sure it got fixed. If an account needed information, he would personally drop it by and review the important details. If his customer was having a long day, he would drop by at 5:00 p.m. and remind them not to work too hard. His customers were so conditioned to his presence that they were surprised when he wasn't there. More importantly, his presence in the office was a way of reassuring them that they were being looked after—*personally* looked after. His customers trusted that assurance and bought from him. He rarely lost to competition because *it never occurred to his customers that they should shop around.*

As fate would have it, he inherited a very nasty account that no other sales rep seemed to have much luck with. The account changed hands constantly as each rep tried in vain to get in and make the quick sale. With each failure came the cascade of excuses:

- The customer is unreasonable.
- The account loves the competition.
- The buyer is working in the Dark Ages.
- The customer just doesn't like us.
- The account hates *all* sales reps.
- They never spend money where they should.
- They are stupid and don't deserve us.

When this high-performing rep took over the account (no one else wanted it), he got plenty of free advice from the other reps: "Don't waste your time—you will never get any business in there. They just won't buy from us."

Undaunted, this rep began his routine of calling and visiting. He spent time in the customer's offices, asking questions and getting to know the people in the trenches. He checked on the one small machine that we still had placed in the far reaches of the building, doing whatever he could to be of help. This rep was approaching the sale in an entirely different way: *He was approaching this customer without a specific sale in mind! He was selling himself first!*

During this period he took a lot of flak from all the other reps who had tried to sell to this account in the past. As far as they were concerned he was flogging a dead horse. But he continued his campaign and soon discovered that this ugly account wasn't so ugly after all. In fact, the customer was so used to being neglected or abused by our company that they welcomed this new salesperson, who didn't even mention the words "promotion" or "deal of a lifetime" or "I'm the new rep and we've really changed the way we work now." For once, a sales rep was willing to take some ownership of his issues without trying to slam a sale at every corner.

The fact is, no one had bothered to go in and *earn* the customer's respect and trust. No one had bothered to build a relationship—no one, that is, until he took over the account. It wasn't long before he got the call he was waiting for. This "customer from hell" left the following message on his voice mail: "Give me a call this week. I think I've got a sale for you."

There is one word at the foundation of every successful customer relationship—and that word is *trust*!

# 45. Every Company Has Its Politics

*"If I were you, I wouldn't put those two in the same room together."*

Imagine that every customer you dealt with was a carbon copy of the character Spock from *Star Trek*. While the conversation might get a little stale, overall it would be fabulous, wouldn't it? Why? Because every sales decision would be based on pure logic. You wouldn't ever have to worry about emotions, pet peeves, hidden agendas, opinions, or moody behavior. On the contrary, decisions would be straightforward, out in the open, and based on pure and simple logic. "Objective selling," we would call it—wouldn't that be nice?

But alas, reality is about selling to real human beings with real agendas. Even the simplest of sales—simple from your point of view—will be complicated by the subjective "human" element. Politics is a good example. We all know and hear about politics. If you live on a planet with more than one human, politicking is pretty much a given.

In selling, politics can really put a twist on the reasons that people buy.

Let me give you an example. I was trying to sell a small photocopier to a nonprofit organization that desperately needed it. Pretty cut and dried, right?

Well no, frankly. One of the buying catalysts wanted to demonstrate her thriftiness by looking at low-cost providers (of course, I was the most expensive game in town). Another one of the buying catalysts was trying to exercise her control over purchasing and, consequently, there was some real friction between the two at every meeting. Finally, the last buying catalyst was most interested in our contributions to non-profit charities—like their own. At the end of the day, not one of the three people gave a hoot about what the photocopier did, and I ended up winning the business because we had strong "friendships" higher up in the organization. In other words, their executive director was a friend of one of our vice-presidents. The only way that I found that out was by receiving a telephone call from our VP's executive assistant telling me to drop my price to well below the lowest price available, no questions asked.

Of course I got the sale, despite the fact that I never met the executive director who signed the order. The other three people involved didn't seem to care and even suggested that most decisions were made that way, so why should they bother putting in any time and effort to help?

Unusual?…bizarre?…incredible?… no, not really. The word I would use to describe that sale is "typical."

Politics is happening at every street corner, in every coffee shop, in every household, and in every one of your accounts. What do you do about it?

Well, try asking questions like:

- Tell me about your political landscape.
- Who would you like to see fired from this organization?
- or (my personal favorite): Are there any unique sexual ties in this organization?

That was all in fun because we all like to think that we are creatures of better judgment, and better judgment steers us away from asking questions that customers clearly would not want to answer.

The solution? Go to your champion (see Chapter 54, "Every Top Performer Has a Champion"). Your success in large organizations will depend on your ability to find and develop at least one champion. Champions can help you navigate through the rough waters of politics. They can tell you who is really making the decisions—and what you should watch out for—before you waste your time selling the wrong benefits to the wrong people.

It's up to you to *position* politics as a positive in your sale. In the end, politics will help you or hurt you, but make no mistake—politics is *always* a factor in large or complex sales.

# 46. You Both Have to Win

*"I wouldn't waste your time in here if I were you. We'll never do business with your company again!"*

Baseball games and courtroom battles have one very important similarity. They define the outcome of a meeting as a "win" or a "loss." In contrast, a sales agreement is a partnership. Each partner gets something from the agreement, and consequently both parties "win." The supplier wins by getting payment for the goods and services provided. The customer wins by getting the end results or benefits of the goods and services received.

Partnerships also differ when it comes to relationships. Unlike rival sports teams or opponents in the courtroom, the two parties in the partnership require an ongoing relationship, sometimes long after the original agreement is signed. Again, both parties enter into the relationship on the assumption that each will profit or "win" over time. The supplier wins through a continuous stream of profitable revenue—in monthly lease or service payments, for example. The customer wins through the ongoing quality and quantity of service and support that the agreement provides for.

The give-and-take nature of a sales agreement is like a marriage.

So, what happens if the marriage doesn't work out? That is, if your customer ends up getting the short end of the stick? In the long run, *you*

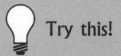

## Try this!

Pick an account that's in bad shape, the result of a bad sales marriage in the recent past. Set up an appointment with the person in the account who got burned and ask them, "What can I do to turn things around?" When the customer gives you their answer (and they will!), tell your customer what you are going to do about it and when you are going to do it. Then make sure that you follow through!

In hindsight, it amazes me how many sales I "won back" by looking after recently burned customers. Even when it was my own company that screwed up, they were thankful that someone was willing to step up to the plate and take care of business. In fact, many customers who first met me feeling anger and frustration became my best customers within a few short months.

*lose too*. For instance, let's say you set some unrealistic delivery and service expectations (in order to win the deal against the competition). In the short term your marriage works. You get your commissions, and the customer gets ready to receive the benefits that they paid for. But look out! When they figure out that they've been duped (that they are on the losing side of the equation), they will soon become the sales marriage from hell: complaints, bad references, lost referrals, excessive maintenance and support, and lost business and missed opportunities will cost you (and your organization) more than you gained.

Now, some people will say that this notion is not "real world"—that is, that you have to do anything and everything to "get the business," even if it means that the customer may not get what they are looking for. In my opinion, that notion still pervades many sales organizations because it is a lot easier to measure success (the price tag of the sale) than it is to measure failure (the cost of complaints, customer service issues, lost future business, etc., etc.). So it becomes much easier for the organization to support the wrong decision.

My advice to you is this: Don't fall into that trap. We all intuitively know that when customers lose, we will ultimately lose as well. So do the right thing for yourself and for the health of the business: Seek and find the place where you both win.

Be good to your sales marriage and remember—"Hell hath no fury like a customer scorned!"

## IN REVIEW

Don't let customers lose at the expense of your win. Those situations have a nasty way of coming back to haunt you (the "what goes around comes around" theory). The issues that surface from customers who lose will often outweigh the benefits you initially receive.

## RECOMMENDED READING

Robert Bruce Miller, Stephen E. Heiman, Diane Sanchez and Tad Tuleja do a good job at discussing the various win/loss scenarios in something they call the "Win-Win Matrix." If you are interested in the subject of "wins," *Strategic Selling*® (New York: Warner Books, 1998) is one book you should read.

# 47. Some Customers Don't Play Fair

*"That customer has hated me from day one! I think he's just one of those people who enjoy treating sales reps like dirt!"*

A wise manager once asked me, "Why are you spending so much time with bad customers?"

You know the type: They're never satisfied with you, they're never straight with you, they're constantly complaining and demanding your personal attention to meaningless details, and their expectations seem to be completely unrealistic. And after all is said and done—after you've broken your back to make them happy—it's still never good enough! Why do we do it?

Well, sometimes we think we need their business. Other times, it's the personal challenge of trying to turn things around. Still, at other times we are reminded that it is just not prudent to walk away from a sale. The truth is, some customers shouldn't be your customers. It's just not a good fit. Their needs and expectations are not a good match to what you have to offer.

Let me give you an example. There is one decision-maker who still gives me shudders when I conjure up her small but commanding image. She essentially ran the show at a very large law firm, a place that needed to copy mountains of paper, and needed it all done yesterday—

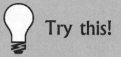

## Try this!

Take your account list back out again. Identify the three worst customers (the three that top the categories of "Will Buy From Us If We're the Cheapest" and "Hard to Do Business With"). With the permission of your sales manager or team leader, stop calling on them and get them off your list!

the perfect fit for Xerox. With a little investigation, it was clear that we were well positioned to meet the firm's needs with our leading-edge technology. Unfortunately, part of this decision-maker's charm and mystique derived from her tenacious belief that old is good. She was the organizational equivalent of a brontosaurus. I wouldn't be surprised if she had her first typewriter and matching rotary phone preserved safely under glass as a memorial to better times.

In a nutshell, her firm needed us, but she did not. And I, oblivious to this fact, spent untold hours courting her and her staff in an effort to find that compelling reason for them to switch to Xerox. After six months and some of the most embarrassing and frustrating meetings of my career (I was insulted, laughed at, yelled at, and practically thrown out), it finally occurred to me: *"Wait a minute—what's wrong with this picture? I have done everything to support them and they've done nothing but torment me!"*

Now, before I get to the big climax, there is a sales manager reading this and thinking, "Keep going, son. Persistence will win. Try some new ideas or talk to some new people. Keep a stiff upper lip and don't give up!"

Normally, I'm all ears to that sort of encouragement, but in this case I was just not reading the writing on the wall (which read: *We are not going to buy from Xerox, come hell or high water. Period. End of statement*). In the meantime, I was spending far too much time with a customer who didn't value what my company had to offer.

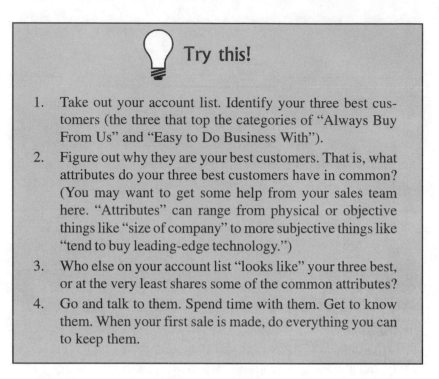

## Try this!

1. Take out your account list. Identify your three best customers (the three that top the categories of "Always Buy From Us" and "Easy to Do Business With").
2. Figure out why they are your best customers. That is, what attributes do your three best customers have in common? (You may want to get some help from your sales team here. "Attributes" can range from physical or objective things like "size of company" to more subjective things like "tend to buy leading-edge technology.")
3. Who else on your account list "looks like" your three best, or at the very least shares some of the common attributes?
4. Go and talk to them. Spend time with them. Get to know them. When your first sale is made, do everything you can to keep them.

The lesson here? When you're faced with a similar situation—that is, when you're caught in the quagmire with a bad customer—stop beating your head against the wall and follow this simple advice: Stop calling on them!

Look at it this way. Every painful moment trying to make a bad customer happy is a moment that could have been spent making a happy customer even happier … and thus making a profitable customer even more profitable.

Don't try to be all things to all people. Spend more of your time making happy customers happier!

## In Review

It makes sense to figure out which customers will be more likely, and more willing, to choose you as their supplier or partner. In my experience, customers who are easy to do business with are often the most profitable.

# Part 11

# Relationships

# 48. Service Your Customers and They'll Remember You

*"The difference between Nancy and all the other reps is that when we leave a message, she always gets right back to us with an answer!"*

I would bet that most of your customers have been through a "reorg." If that's true, there is a good chance they've been downsized, right-sized, outsourced, streamlined, empowered, flattened, and/or teamed to death. And it's no secret that the post-reorganization work environment is often about doing more with less. What does all that mean to you? Well, it means that your customers need you now, more than ever—whether they care to admit it or not. They need you because they can't do it alone anymore. There's too much to do. Too many changes. Too few staff. Too little budget ...

Customers need help!

That's one of the reasons why these days you hear so much about strategic alliances, value-added resellers, business consultants, outsourcing, and partnerships. So it should come as no surprise, then, that successful sellers understand the importance of service; in other words, *successful sellers are there to help!* And how do you spot a salesperson who does a good job servicing customers? Well, chances are you won't. You see, these reps aren't hanging around the office. They're with their customers. They're *"servicing"*!

And what is "servicing"? It's a lot of things, really. Mostly it's talking to customers and spending time with them. It's learning about their operations so that you can anticipate their problems and concerns. It's being around them when problems crop up, or better still, being around early enough to help stop problems before they occur.

Servicing is a helpful spreadsheet, an unexpected drop-in, and a returned voice mail. It's babysitting a temperamental product, analyzing a confusing bill, and sending the customer an interesting magazine article "FYI." Servicing might even be a rush delivery and a cup of coffee. Frankly, it can be any number of things that demonstrate that you're on the job and that you care about them and their business.

The result? Contrary to popular belief, hard work does pay off and, in my experience, servicing customers builds strong relationships. Also, contrary to popular belief, a strong relationship, even in highly competitive and price-sensitive markets, can be the primary reason a customer chooses one vendor over another. Why? Because if the customer thinks that you are working for them, then you are something they desperately need: somebody they can depend on! That's becoming a rare commodity these days, and as rare commodities go, dependable people are difficult to find and harder to keep! So when customers *find* you, they're going to want to *keep* you, even if it means paying a little more.

One last thought on servicing. Something that sales organizations are hard pressed to admit is that there is usually very little "perceived" difference between products and services among competitors in highly "mature" and competitive marketplaces. How, then, is the customer to make the difficult decision of choosing between competitive bids? Believe me, when it comes down to the crunch, and everybody's proposal is starting to look the same, customers will often fall back on the one thing that they know best … the one thing that is closest to them … the relationship! *"Who do I really trust to get the job done?"* Of course, if you've played your cards right, you hope the answer is you!

*Good sales reps don't talk "service"—they do it!*

# 49. Don't Spend Too Much Time Fighting Fires

*"I don't know how I'm going to make quota. I spend half my time reacting to customer complaints and the other half fixing them!"*

Wouldn't it be great if you had just one customer and your sole task in life was to make them happy? Unfortunately, selling involves many customers with many ongoing problems. You could spend weeks looking after every one of those issues without really doing much selling. It's easy to do. Customers will often want to drag their trusty sales rep back into the fold when things have gone awry, and that means you're on the hook for getting everything back on track.

So, let's clarify this idea of "servicing" the customer.

Servicing your customers does *not* mean "putting out all their fires." Chances are, your company is not paying you to fight fires because they have other people to do that (that is, customer service, billing, administration, credit, etc.). If you doubt me on this one, take a look at how your performance is measured from month to month. If there is no measurement for how many fires you put out, but there is a measurement for sales revenue—well, you get the idea.

Your job is to "service" your customers in a way that no one else in your organization can. It is your job to "service" the "relationship." That means you are the fire chief, not the firefighter. At most, your role is to coordinate firefighting activities so that your time can be better

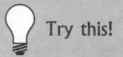 Try this!

When your customer has said yes to your solution—with the appropriate signature or approval—set their expectations for your role as the "fire chief" in the relationship. Here are some simple guidelines:

1. The basic premise: Leave firefighting to the rest of your organization. Your job is to sell.

2. Get to know every one of your firefighters personally and treat them like gold!

3. With the sales agreement in place, explain that you are "stepping out" of the "implementation" phase of the process and "handing off" this phase to your implementation team (your firefighters). Introduce your firefighting team to the customer and introduce yourself as the "fire chief" (or quarterback, orchestrator, etc.). Explain the difference between the two—that it is your role to understand the business issues (the "business development" phase) and to bring the appropriate resources to bear on those issues. If possible, have your customers call your team directly; after all, they are so much better at firefighting than you are ("and besides, you'll just get my voice mail!").

4. Plan to make periodic calls to your customer and your firefighting team(s) to make sure that "all is well" (an ounce of prevention ... ).

5. Choose to "service" your customers, when "service"
   • is mostly proactive.
   • strengthens the relationship.
   • advances a sale.

spent building and strengthening the relationships between you and your customers. You will need those relationships if you are to strengthen your position for sales today and in the future.

*A seller's job is to sell—not to fight fires.*

## IN REVIEW

Firefighting is a big issue for salespeople. On the one hand, putting out fires is not your job, but on the other hand, you still have to make sure that the fires are out and that your customer is happy. Therefore, while it is not your job to service the fires; it is your job to service the relationship. Ensure your customer understands this. Be proactive and tell them!

# 50. Know Your Customer's Customer

*"We started using their service because most of our customers were using them."*

Lots of people are talking about the "value chain" these days. But what exactly is it, and what has it got to do with selling? For me, the value chain illustrates the important components or "links" in your customer's business cycle (inputs and outputs). In its most basic form, it looks something like this:

**INPUT**                                              **OUTPUT**

Bob's Parts          Sally's Engines          Jim's Fine Cars

In the above automobile example, Bob (a car part manufacturer) sells his car parts to Sally (a car engine assembler), who in turn sells the whole engine to Jim (an auto manufacturer).

A good sales rep who is selling to Sally will ask her about her business issues, and then provide a recommendation that will solve those issues. If, for example, you were in the business of speeding up assembly lines with high-tech robotics, you would be wise to investigate Sally's issues and needs concerning assembly-line efficiency and productivity.

Today, however, there is a new breed of major account sales representative out there who will take it a step further. This salesperson will look at Bob's and Jim's operations to understand what Sally's assembly-line efficiency and productivity issues mean to them. Now, you might be asking, "Why would any rep go to that much trouble?"

The answer is in the recommendation. The sales rep who makes a proposal to address just one customer will be fixing only one link in the value chain or, in this case, Sally's assembly operations. If that rep does a good job, Sally will certainly be impressed by the expected improved efficiency of her assembly line: "Sally, with our new robotics products, your assembly line will see efficiency and productivity gains of 15 percent overall."

Now, 15 percent is nothing to sneeze at, but my guess is that Sally cares more about the *effect* that a 15 percent improvement will have on acquiring or improving her relationships with her customers and suppliers. Why? Well, without her suppliers she has nothing to build, and without her customers she has nothing to sell. So imagine the look on her face when the second salesperson tells her that they have investigated her suppliers and customers to determine which robotic solution would make the best sense for the whole chain: "Sally, if you implement our robotics solution, Bob will be able to use a more popular and available car part that will make his life easier and reduce costs for both of you. At Jim's end, not only will he get the engines sooner, but Bob's new part is twice as reliable, which means that Jim will be making a better car. I checked it out with Jim and he agreed, but he also told me that the added time-to-market gains would be a big plus for him. . . Oh, and by the way, I should add that you can expect assembly-line efficiency and productivity gains of 15 percent."

Who do you think is better positioned to win Sally's business?

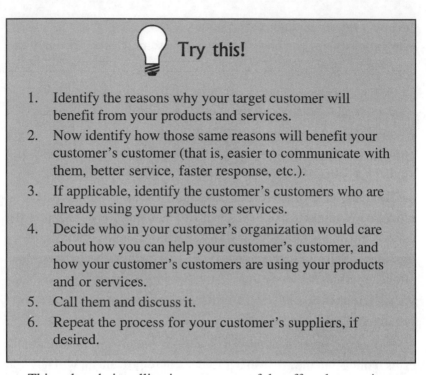

**Try this!**

1. Identify the reasons why your target customer will benefit from your products and services.
2. Now identify how those same reasons will benefit your customer's customer (that is, easier to communicate with them, better service, faster response, etc.).
3. If applicable, identify the customer's customers who are already using your products or services.
4. Decide who in your customer's organization would care about how you can help your customer's customer, and how your customer's customers are using your products and or services.
5. Call them and discuss it.
6. Repeat the process for your customer's suppliers, if desired.

This value chain selling is pretty powerful stuff, so let me give you another example, but this time a real one. A good friend of mine is a high-performing salesperson in a very large telecommunications company. He manages what is frequently called a "vertical" assignment—the health vertical—which means that all of his customers are in the health industry. ("Horizontal" assignments have accounts from all types of industries.) With only one business focus, it didn't take him long to understand the needs of this unique industry (suppliers, competitors, and end customers).

He had this one particular customer—a large hospital—and he grew to understand this customer's value chain very well. But that knowledge wasn't enough for him. He knew that telecommunications was an important link in the chain, and so it wasn't long before he began making sales calls on his customer's customers. Let me be clear on this point. He actually went out and talked to his customer's customers—local heathcare companies—to understand how telecommunications was being used by them. From his efforts emerged a profound and unique understanding of the telecommunications environment across the entire chain. It was an understanding that no previous rep had ever thought to uncover. Can you imagine the credibility of his proposal? It outlined how the network of health-care providers was going to benefit from the hospital's improved communications. His proposal actually showed the link between telecommunications and improved customer relationships and profitability.

His customer signed the agreement.

So why did he go to such lengths? Well, it's simple: He needed some really good reasons to justify a very large and long-term sales contract. But my friend also used his value chain–selling strategy to subtly lock out the competition. In fact, the cost of his solution was never an issue, and no serious competitor ever rose to the challenge, despite the multimillion-dollar opportunity the sale represented. The customer just never thought of shopping around, and here's why: My sales friend knew that his customer's customers and his customer's suppliers were already using his telecommunications products and services, so it seemed only natural that the customer would follow suit and integrate with the rest of the chain.

Do you have any customers like that? Customers whose suppliers and/or end customers are already using your products and services? Check it out!

To sum up, value chain selling is an advanced art, but it can help you build major credibility with your customers and lock out potential competitors. It's not for everybody because it can take a lot of extra time and effort, and if you have hundreds of accounts it's probably just not practical to be calling on your customers' customers and suppliers. But even in this situation, there are aspects of value chain selling that can help you. You can start by considering, and then asking questions about, your customers' value chain. Your customers will be impressed by your "systems" approach to selling, and you will be able to get a much clearer picture of the real value you can bring to their organizations.

## In Review

You may want to know who your customers' suppliers and customers are because your knowledge of their "value chain" will help you understand what is and what isn't important to your customers. It's not hard, but it does require some additional time and effort. You should be doing this if you plan on taking "selling" to a more strategic level with an important or very large customer. You should also be doing this if the suppliers or customers are happily using your products and services.

## About Value

There are plenty of books about "value" out there. Considering the amount of discussion that the word "value" tends to generate, I think it is a good idea to get a solid foundation in the following value terms: value, value chain, value selling, and value propositions. (In my opinion, value is something that a customer is willing to pay for. End of story.)

# 51. "Inside" Customers Are Important, Too

*"Our customer support team is useless!"*

I once watched in horror as a tenured salesperson—unhappy about a service-related problem—started screaming at a service representative, much to the embarrassment of everyone nearby. Oddly enough, just moments before her tirade she was calmly talking on the phone, trying to pacify an unhappy customer. On that telephone call, her voice was full of empathy, sincerity, and helpfulness. But by the time the phone was back in its cradle, rage was steaming from both ears. Her Jekyll and Hyde performance that day demonstrated a common and regrettable belief: Treat your external customers like gold, and no one else really matters.

Not true!

Think about the repercussions of that event. Regardless of the reason, a service rep was humiliated in front of other employees. Word will spread of that deed and soon the reputation of the salesperson will precede her. The next time her customer is in a pinch, who do you think will save the day? The service rep who took the hard knocks? I doubt it.

The point is this. No one adheres to job descriptions anymore. As salespeople, we depend on our whole organization to do whatever it takes to make (and keep) our customers happy. Translation: The parts

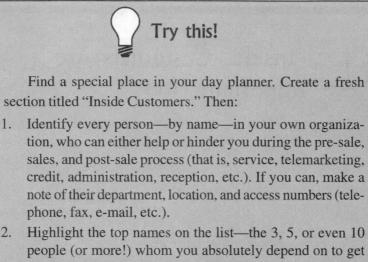

## Try this!

Find a special place in your day planner. Create a fresh section titled "Inside Customers." Then:

1. Identify every person—by name—in your own organization, who can either help or hinder you during the pre-sale, sales, and post-sale process (that is, service, telemarketing, credit, administration, reception, etc.). If you can, make a note of their department, location, and access numbers (telephone, fax, e-mail, etc.).
2. Highlight the top names on the list—the 3, 5, or even 10 people (or more!) whom you absolutely depend on to get the job of selling done. Try to imagine your day without these people. Now, call the top people on your list and make it clear how much you appreciate them.

of your organization that look after your customers are "internal customers"—*your* internal customers!

What would you do without them? They're the ones who bail you out of annoying and time-intensive service issues, or who take that important phone call because your customer has grown tired of your voice mail message and wants to talk with somebody "live," or who fix your sales order paperwork that would otherwise sit on hold for who knows how long. And they're the ones who help you sell to an account by supporting your proposal, or spotting an opportunity that you were not there to see.

A last word. When that sales rep goes looking for that service person to help her in a time of need, the service rep will be nowhere to be found. The service rep will be out looking after the customers of those sales reps who treat their colleagues as they would their best customers.

"No man is an island."

## IN REVIEW

You need your inside customers (the people in your own organization) just as much as your outside customers. You depend on them. They depend on you.

# 52. Some Customers Need You More than Others

*"I don't get it. They've been with us forever. But it's like pulling teeth to get an appointment with these guys."*

At some point you are going to walk into an established customer's office for a comfortable visit. While the official purpose is to check on customer satisfaction, the real reason is to lay your claim to a great victory—to bask in the glory of your accomplishments. And why not? This customer is one of the good ones: easy to do profitable business with, reasonable and loyal, and one who has twice provided a glowing reference for you. Best of all, this customer just signed a landmark deal that brought you the recognition, respect, and reward that you deserve.

Much to your surprise, this "best" customer of yours does not want to see you. You head back to your office. You make calls that are not returned. The customer is just not interested in you anymore.

Now this must be some kind of mistake! After all, it was only two months ago that you signed the paperwork. Everyone was smiles and handshakes then. Now, your repeated attempts to reconnect with your key contacts are fruitless. No one has any time on their calendars for you. So, after a few repeat calls, and with a hint of frustration in your voice, you resign yourself to a simple cold, hard fact: "I'm yesterday's news!"

Congratulations: You have just experienced rejection without actually being rejected.

Here's why. There are lots of customers out there who think that buying and selling is a necessary evil. They might get along with salespeople and realize their importance, but they only want to involve salespeople when it's time to buy something. There's a term for customers like that—"transaction-based." They see a purchase as a static moment in time, and you are only a conduit to the products and services they need.

Don't take it personally. It's just their buying style.

Here's an easy idea to work with. When you get to know a client a little better, or even at the beginning of a relationship, step outside the traditional questioning sequence and ask your customer one of these questions:

- How would you like to work together?
- What do you value in a vendor-client relationship?
- What role do you see me playing in your buying process?

All customers will appreciate such questions, and it's my guess that few salespeople ask them.

Now, back to your transaction-based customer. I wish there were a tactic or magic potion that could make this issue go away, but the truth of the matter is that transaction-based customers are out there, and there isn't a whole lot you can do about it.

Don't worry. Work with your transaction-based customers the way they wish (according to their answers to the above questions), and spend your time nurturing the "relationship" customers. Those are the customers who have accepted the necessity and value of developing strong relationships with their vendors. Those are the ones who will value your visits, your timely information mailings, your phone mail updates, etc.

The two types of customers have something in common: There is a way to treat them and a way not to treat them, and the only way you will know for sure is to ask!

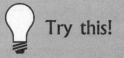 **Try this!**

With an existing customer, or even a brand-new one, finish off your telephone or sales call with this nontraditional sales question: "How should we work together on this?"

A word of warning: Some customers will be taken aback by this question because in my experience few sales reps think to ask it. So here are some alternative wordings:

- How often should I be calling on you?
- Do you like to be kept up to date on all of the latest developments?
  What do you value in a salesperson?
- Do you like to golf?

Try whatever you feel is appropriate. Your customers will appreciate it!

## IN REVIEW

Different customers want different things from their vendor-supplier relationships. On one hand, there are those customers who want constant contact with their sellers because they value the relationship. On the other hand, there are those customers who want very little to do with sellers; they are annoyed by sales calls and would rather not talk to any salespeople until it is time to buy something. Chances are, you have customers who are at both ends of the spectrum and lots in the middle, and that means that you can't treat them all as equals.

# 53. One Really Good Contact Isn't Good Enough

*"It's a done deal! John always buys from Xerox."*

I cringe when I see that particular quote because it illustrates the very real danger of a sticking to a single good contact.

Here is a case study from my past. I had been working on a very large advertising agency for a number of months, and was feeling very confident that I would get the "big sale" in short order. We had an expression for those types of prospects; we called them "done deals." My confidence was based on my relationship with one individual in the account. This guy loved Xerox. He would do anything for me if it meant increasing the odds of a sale, which I think was best illustrated when he gave me a copy of a competitive spread sheet so that I would be more prepared to beat them. (That's about as good as it gets.) This guy wanted me to win, and the "brass" upstairs always went with his recommendation.

Then one foggy Christmas day … I picked up a very disturbing voicemail message. My reconnaissance man, my support mechanism, my product worshipper, my champion of champions—was fired from his job! And my $90,000 deal went right out the door with him.

Hedge your bets: *Get to know as many buying catalysts as you can!*

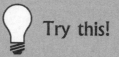 **Try this!**

The next time you visit this "one really good contact," ask, "Who else in your organization would support our company in your absence?"

If they are strong enough advocates for you, they should provide a few new contacts for you, but make sure that you ask for their blessing to have you, or someone else in your organization, begin to establish a new relationship in the account.

If they don't want you calling anywhere else, find out why and then get somebody else in your own organization to make a call on your behalf.

## IN REVIEW

Very often, we rely on one really good contact in our account because they have always been there for us in the past. Unfortunately, nothing lasts forever, and salespeople who fail to develop multiple relationships can find themselves out of a sale and even out of an account if their one good contact gets up and walks out the door.

# 54. Every Top Performer Has a Champion

*"Thank God for Beverly. If she wasn't my best customer, I'd hire her."*

Not long ago I was asked to facilitate a focus group of 14 top-performing salespeople. The group was brought together on this particular day to compare notes on their best victories and worst defeats (a process we called "war stories"), and it was my job to spot similarities among the presentations. Sure enough, there was one trend that was hard to miss—the presence or absence of a kind of customer we often called the "champion."

Every one of the 14 best victories enjoyed the presence of one. Every one of the fourteen worst defeats suffered the absence of one. Coincidence? I don't think so!

In the discussions that followed each presentation, it wasn't hard to see why the accounts presented were given the status of "best" victory. None of the 14 reps picked an easy or small account to qualify. On the contrary, these accounts were big and often confusing. These accounts were sold complicated and broad-based solutions. These accounts were mired in controversy because of something we did, or didn't do. These accounts were either strongly positioned with a worthy competitor, or the competition was nipping at our heels. These accounts had a long, treacherous, and ever-changing sales cycle, fraught with many obstacles, frustrations, and disappointments.

These accounts had it all: complexity, diversity, and hostility. So, in each and every case, the wise group of fourteen headed into the quagmire with one prevailing thought: *"I can't do this alone."*

Each rep found, developed, and nurtured a customer "champion"— a person inside the organization who could help them sell. Focusing on this one person, they sold themselves, their products and services, and their company. When they had accomplished that feat, a champion was born—and then the real fun began.

- The champion provided valuable insight on the tricky political waters in the organization.
- The champion guided the sales rep as to which contacts were the most important and who really made the decision.
- The champion called the sales rep with the latest change in the organization.
- The champion offered information on "who liked whom," and why that would matter.
- The champion told the rep which competitors were on the scene and how to beat them.
- The champion got the rep the appointment that was the turning-point of the sale.
- The champion graciously accepted the lunch invitation or the tickets to the game as a thank-you for the multimillion-dollar sale.

Does that sound like someone who would be handy to have in your sales?

Of course! But who qualifies as the champion?—because not just anyone will do. For openers, a true champion believes in your solution. Where does that belief come from? Most of the champions that I have developed believed in me because I could fix one of their fires (see Chapter 34, "Find the Fires"). I have also found that champions value the relationship; that is, there is "something in it for them" to help you. Either way—the value of the relationship or the value of your solution—there must be a reason that your champion is your champion. Why? Because no one is going to support your proposal out of the goodness of their heart. Life is just not that convenient.

**Try this!**

If you think that you have a good champion (they support your solution), it's perhaps time that you tested your assumption. When you two are talking next, ask him or her what they like about your solution and why he or she would want to support it. Good champions will give you a direct answer to that question. Bad champions will skate around the answer, and that means you may be putting too much faith in them!

Here's the last big point on champions. Chances are, you spend only a fraction of your time actually selling to any one customer. The remainder of your time is divided among other customers and other time-robbing activities like travel, paperwork, meetings, and so on.

But your champion is always in your account, and therefore is always close to the action.

To sum up:

... Find your champion!

... Develop your champion!

... Leverage your champion!

## IN REVIEW

A champion is someone in your account who is a strong supporter of your solution. They can provide you with a wealth of information that in large and difficult sales can make the difference between success and failure. They will only provide that information if they truly value your relationship and the solution that you are proposing (there is "something in it for them"). Successful sellers develop champions.

Unsuccessful sellers do not.

# Part

## Proposing

# 55. What Your Product "Does" Is Not Important

*"It slices, it dices, it Julienne-fries ..."*

Not many people look forward to actually shopping for a toaster—but lots of people love to eat toast!

Imagine a toaster salesperson describing with infinite detail the reasons their toaster is the one for you:

*No, please wait! You have to hear this! The heating elements are independently charged and come with an advanced cool-down feature that actually responds to minute changes in the electromagnetic field. Don't go away, there's more. Because of the safety features of this system, the shell of the unit actually remains at room temperature, while the uniform heat distribution system ensures even cooking and...*

The bad news for this toaster salesperson is that the customer standing on the receiving end of this dissertation didn't really care about the heating technology or the safety features, and was thinking: "Listen, buddy, all I want is an affordable toaster that will match the color of my kitchen."

The truth is, too many salespeople talk for too long about things that don't matter to their customers.

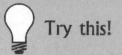 **Try this!**

Here's a good exercise for a new product or service.

List the top three features of your latest and greatest product or service offering (that is, small and sleek toaster design). Beside each feature, indicate what that feature "does" for everyone using it (that is, it fits conveniently and looks good in a contemporary kitchen).

Now, write down both the name of a customer who will benefit from the features, and what they do (their business). The challenge is to put yourself in your customer's shoes (the person who is going to buy it). Do they really care about the stuff you've just written down? Are they willing to pay for what this product or service "does" as you have just described it? (Do they value the fit and good looks of the toaster?)

If the answer is yes, pat yourself on the back. If the answer is maybe, try the exercise again, but this time take yourself out of it! Try to write down the feature and what the feature "does" as if you were your customer doing this same exercise.

If you can get in the habit of preparing your thoughts and words with your customers in mind, chances are you will be much more effective in making presentations that your customers will want to hear.

The solution is simple. Salespeople should forget about what their products or services do *for everybody* and focus on what their products and services do *for their specific customer*. It slices, dices, and Julienne-fries is only important when the customer needs it. It's as simple as that.

So, before you get all hyped up about the latest and greatest thing that your organization cooks up, think about what approach your colleagues in sales are going to take. The low performers will rush out and start telling the world about how great your new stuff is. *"It's faster, it's better, it's cleaner, it's more seamless, it's less faulty, it's longer-lasting ..." "It's this and it's that ..."* Notice how the focus is on the product or service?

Your high-performing peers will translate the latest and greatest into how it will solve their customers' problems.[†] *"Because of the increased speed, you will be able to ... Its seamless integration with existing systems means that your operations people can ..."* Here the focus is on the customer—and those customers listen.

Remember this: It's your job to translate what a product does into *why* the customer would care.

So when your company introduces the next "latest and greatest" product or service, consider this question: *For Customer X, what does it do for their business?*

## IN REVIEW

What your product does is not important. What effect that product has on your customer's business is all that really matters.

# 56. The Cost of the Problem Must Outweigh the Cost of the Solution

*"American Express Travelers checks: Don't leave home without them!"*

Why do you buy travelers checks? Is it because they are convenient? Maybe. Is it because you want to protect your cash? Could be. But if you are to believe the television commercials, the reason you buy American Express travelers checks is because the cost of purchasing the checks is far less than the cost of ruining your vacation.

The same premise works for Volvo: The cost of the new car is far less than the cost of personal accident injury.

And then there's Michelin: The cost of the tires is far less than the cost of an injured child.

So how does this apply to your selling? Well, building on our chapter about problems (see Chapter 36, "A Problem Is Only a Problem When the Customer Thinks It's a Problem"), let's say that your customer agrees with your perception of the problem. Is it time to rush back to your desk and begin putting together the proposal?

Well, that depends on the size of the problem. Is the problem big enough to warrant the cost of a solution? (Is the vacation important enough to warrant the cost of the travelers checks?)

Here's an interesting little fact. Not long ago some wise people decided to survey a group of customers to find out about their buying motivations. When asked "At what point do you make the decision to buy?" many of the customers responded: "When the cost of not doing anything about my problems outweighs the cost of fixing them."

That's because our customers typically have lots of problems and limited resources (many fires but only so much water). It's as though they have a hole in the roof, a furnace on the fritz, and windows that won't keep out the rain, but the budget to fix their house will only allow for one of those solutions, at least in the short term. Which one would you fix first?

To sum up: In a world of multiple problems, limited resources, and rapid change, customers have to be careful about where and when they invest in solutions. They're always looking to get the "biggest bang for the buck."

That means that the problems that you can solve for your customer are competing for attention with all kinds of other problems that may be more pressing, and more costly, in the mind of your customer. What do you do about it?

Why, you ask questions, of course. You ask questions to explore the costs of the issues pertaining to your solution. If you do a good job at assigning a price tag to the true size and scope of their problems, your customer will begin to think that the cost of the solution is worth it. ("Let's fight this fire first!") Back to our house example.

If you were the roof salesman, you might explore the long-term costs of water damage and roof rot. ("What effect is that hole having on the rest of your roof?") You may explore the implications and the inherent dangers of the natural materials like dirt and water that will enter the home. ("What impact are these materials having on the inside of your house?") You might even talk about the costs of animals' entering the house and doing damage, plus the cost of removal. (Raccoon vacation property?) Your ability to explore the size and cost of that hole will begin to make the customer realize the need to fix it. Once again,

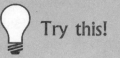 Try this!

Pick an account of yours that is somewhere in the "evaluating problem(s)" stage. To qualify, this customer should be interested in the problem, but is not yet ready to pay anybody to fix it.

Now the tricky part. (This may require a fair amount of work.) Your task is to answer this question: What would it "cost" your customer to not fix the problem? In other words, how much does it cost your customer to live with this problem? You may use hard-dollar (objective) or soft-dollar (subjective) costs; but when all is said and done, when your list is complete, you must be able to show that the cost of the problem warrants the cost of the solution.

Now here's an even trickier part. Does your customer know and accept the true costs of the problem, or are they living in ignorant bliss? If they don't know what you know, then what questions will you ask your customer to help them discover the true cost(s) of the problem? (Remember, as a seller, you can't "tell" people that their problems are costly.) Customers don't like to be shown holes in the operation by some outsider or, worse, by a sales rep. But you can help them draw their own conclusions on the basis of the answers to questions that you will ask! (See Chapter 7, "Use Your Natural Curiosity to Get the Answers.")

When you have given enough thought to the costs and to the questions you will ask your customer to uncover them, get on the telephone and book an appointment. It's time your customer recognized that this problem of theirs should go to the top of their priority list. Good luck.

the secret of selling is in the questions that you ask of your customers. The key is to ask questions that get your customers thinking and talking about the true size (cost) of their problems.

*Customers with costly problems will be motivated to fix them.*

## In review

Customers are motivated to fix their problems when they see that the cost of the problem justifies the expense of the solution.

## Recommended reading

This chapter comes right from Huthwaite's research. For a more in-depth look at the subject of problems and their costs, I suggest that you read, embrace, and practice the art of *Spin Selling* by Neil Rackham (New York: McGraw-Hill, 1996).

# 57. Don't Put Too Much Faith in Your Nice-Looking Proposal

*"My client had better appreciate all the work that went into that proposal!"*

Over the years I have visited a lot of busy customers whose work environment looked more like a war zone than an office. Messy desks and offices are often a good topic for light conversation, and customers will be quick to tell you about their helter-skelter life of "too much to do … and too little time."

But look closer.

Amid the litter of internal paperwork, letters, memos, and the like are a few proposals lying in wait. These are the work of diligent sales reps who have come before you. Sometimes I will find myself staring at a lonesome proposal, and I imagine the author waiting outside in the bushes, where they have been sitting for the past three or four months—desperate but hopeful. Of course, the customer has long since forgotten about that salesperson, not to mention their discarded work of brilliance. The proposal, and all the work that went into it, has long since been swallowed up by the confusion on the desk: its content, context, and meaning all lost.

In my opinion, too many proposals end up this way, cast aside by customers who do not have the time or inclination to read them. Why is that?

Part of the answer comes from a phenomenon that I believe pervades many sales organizations. It is the belief that the sales proposal is the Holy Grail of sales tools—the pride, joy, and benchmark of the organization, and the written affirmation that will snatch victory from the jaws of defeat.

Nonsense.

Yes, proposals are important. They should be the written confirmation of everything you have discussed. Also, proposals represent you and your company long after you have left. Often they are the only selling vehicle that make it to the top of the decision tree, so they most definitely have an importance. But before you go and get your knickers in a knot over your latest work of art, ask yourself these three questions:

1. *Did I get the customer's agreement to consider my proposal seriously?* How often do we run away and write up a proposal because it seems like the logical thing to do! Is your customer ready to look at your proposal? Are they serious about this? Do they have the money? Do they have the resources? Are they ready to buy or are they just kicking tires?

2. *Have I asked my customer what this proposal should look like?* Do they like an executive summary? Do they want a covering letter? Do they want a lot of detail or only the key points? Should you put technical support materials in an appendix? So often we try to guess what the customer would like, or worse, we assume that our gift for writing proposals will be admired by all who lay eyes on it.

3. *Who else is going to look at it?* Hey, presumably those who read your proposal will be offering their opinion on it. In other words, they may have an influence on your sale. Is there any way you can talk to those decision "catalysts" before you write the proposal so that you can tailor it to them? Are they looking for something different? Are they for you or against you? Should you write a separate proposal for them because they want to see different things, or the same things written in a different way (an executive versus a technical support person)?

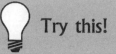 Try this!

When you are ready to present your next proposal, do yourself a favor and ask yourself these three questions:

1. Is my customer serious? Are they ready to see this proposal (are they in a buying window?) or is this just a "spray and pray"?

2. Have I asked my customer what they would like to see in this proposal, or is this just my own creative approach?

3. Do I know who is going to read it, or at least have some input? Do I know what they are looking for in this proposal?

The answers to those questions will help you deliver a superior and customer-centered proposal. The big pearl of wisdom here? Understand first...propose second.

To sum up:
- Ask your customers if they are ready and serious about your proposal.
- Write it up the way they would like to see it.
- Make sure there is something in it for everyone who reads it.

*Write proposals for customers who want to read them.*

## IN REVIEW

A nice-looking or elaborate proposal usually won't make the big difference in the sale, particularly if the customer wasn't involved in creating it. Proposals should never be a surprise to your customer. Proposals should simply be a written validation of everything that the customer and seller have discussed thus far. Finally, proposals should be written as your customer would like to read them.

# 58. Customers Who Call You for Help May Not Want Any

*"They haven't said a word to us in two years and now all of a sudden they want a quote."*

If you were trying to sell something and you knew that your customer was going to shop around, who would you suggest they talk to? Well, many reps would point to their weaker competitors or a smaller competitor, or to a more expensive competitor. Why? *To make themselves look good in the face of their competition.*

So if you get a call for a quote that seems, well, "out of the blue," especially if the customer has otherwise never given you the time of day—look out! You are probably being "benchmarked." Your competitor, or even your customer, has suggested that their proposal be compared to your proposal, with the idea that yours will only strengthen the merit of theirs.

Don't do it! Don't respond as they have requested! There's nothing to be gained by it! Ask for an appointment to explore the customer's business needs so that you can be sure to make the right recommendation for them—a recommendation that positions your products and services against your competitors'. If the customer says no, then they can't possibly be serious about you. So you should politely decline.

If you get pressure from your own organization to provide a proposal anyway (some companies make it a policy to respond to all requests for proposals), don't despair. You still have "writer's control," so please take this advice: Propose some very vague options and very wide price ranges. If you play your cards right, your proposal will not allow for competitive benchmarking, but will pique your customer's curiosity: *"Some of their ideas and options are interesting. Perhaps we should stop the presses and let these folks come in and give us a real quote."*

Don't give your competitors the edge. Get in there and sell your proposal!

Part  13

Concerns

# 59. Successful Objection Handlers Understand What the Customer Is Trying to Say

*"I couldn't close him. He said he had to think about it. I hate that objection!"*

Let's face it: Objections can be frustrating and disappointing. After all, they're a customer's way of saying no to you—usually at the most crucial time of the sale—when you're at the final commitment. Right?

Hold on a minute! An objection is *not* the same thing as a no. In my experience, customers who say no tend to leave a voice mail and say, "Sorry, but we decided to hold off and buy next year," or perhaps write a "Thanks, but no thanks" letter or e-mail, and be done with it. Some customers don't even bother to return phone calls, hoping that the sales rep will get the message and stop calling them. (Ouch!)

But if the customer is not saying no and they're certainly not saying yes, then what are they saying?

They're saying stop.

Customers take inherent risks when buying a product or service. These risks surface mostly at the end of the sales cycle because it is time to actually put their money where their mouth is, and that means taking the ultimate risk—the risk of purchase. During the selling process, when they are talking to you, or giving you access to the organization, or reviewing an initial proposal, customers are not as likely to object because it's all free. Your long and hard work selling costs the customer nothing—until, that is, you ask for the order. At that point, everything changes. You and your proposal are going to carry a big price tag. And in the customer's mind, cost equals risk.

Customers have to ask themselves, "Is the benefit of this change worth the risk?" It's kind of a professional gamble with you as the dealer and your customer wondering whether it's worth betting the farm to see the next card. That's why customers put up stop signs; they want to make sure that the risk is worth it. So don't look upon an objection as a no, but rather as a question—a question about the benefit or the risk.

And it's a question that needs an answer before you move along with the matter at hand. Sometimes the objection (question) is based on missing information that you will need to provide. (*I can't go ahead with this until I know more about the product's specifications.*) Sometimes it's an objection (question) based on a misunderstanding that you will need to clarify. (*I'm a little concerned about the small size of your service organization; I'm afraid we won't get the service and response we need.*) Sometimes the objection (question) is a smokescreen (an excuse for something else)—it's not really true or relevant—but it's easier for the customer to use as a way to get rid of you rather than admit the truth (that is, *you're too expensive* when the customer is really thinking, *I've heard that your service is lousy*). Sometimes it's a completely irrational objection (question) that has no relevance to the sale or is just a rehashed issue that you dealt with a long time ago (customers can become somewhat irrational at this risky, and even scary, point of the selling process).

Regardless, your success will not be measured by the speed of your response but by whether you understand the true nature of the concern. Is there really a problem? Is there a misunderstanding? Is the question a smokescreen for underlying issues? Is your customer expressing an irrational fear?

Don't react. Don't get upset. Don't guess. Stop. Listen. And acknowledge the customer's fear or concern. Most important, find out

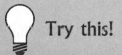

## Try this!

Take some time to create the "Dirty Dozen"—a list of the twelve most dreaded objections that you can think of, the ones that you hope and pray you will never hear at the end of a sale (or maybe at the beginning of the sale).

When you are satisfied with your list—satisfied that you have indeed collected the quintessential Dirty Dozen—a list that would make even your sales manager or VP shudder, it's time to assemble the panel of experts.

Go to your veteran sales reps, the best and brightest in your organization, and ask them to respond to your objections. Make sure you take notes because different reps will handle the objections in different ways.

When it comes to the Dirty Dozen, it's always best to hear it from the pros first. You want to be prepared for the time that you hear it from your biggest customer, during your biggest sale.

the true nature of the objection. Customer: "*I would like to think about it.*" You: "*I realize that there are a lot of details on the table here, so perhaps I can help you. What do you need to think about before you can make your decision?*"

Consider your customer's point of view. Would you want to deal with a sales rep who tried to sweep objections quickly under the carpet without really understanding your concerns? Would it worry you that a sales rep got nervous when answering you? Or would you like to deal with a calm and collected sales rep who took the time to understand your true issues and then deal with them?

The secret to objections is *understanding* first, and *responding* second.

# IN REVIEW

Objections are not a rejection. They are merely questions that need an answer. Unfortunately, they often come at the point when the sale is to be concluded, when the risks for the buyer and seller are high (risk of purchase versus risk of sale). Too many sales reps become emotional and try to "stamp out" objections too quickly, out of fear of losing the sale. Resist the urge to react. The secret to objections is clarifying your customer's question first! Is it a misunderstanding? A smokescreen? A drawback? Find out, and then respond.

# RECOMMENDED READING

Once again, I refer you to the research of Neil Rackham—this time in his *Major Account Sales Strategy* (New York: McGraw-Hill, 1989). The book gives you a lot to think about, both about the subject of objections and about the bigger picture, which he calls "Resolution of Concerns."

# 60. Get to the Real Issues— Isolate the Objection

*"I find it hard to believe that she's stalling because of the price. Are you sure that's the reason?"*

Get yourself into the healthy habit of isolating objections. Why? Because when I hear: "You're too expensive," my spider senses start tingling. In my experience, customers who bring out the "ol' price objection" are often using it as a smokescreen. What they're really saying is "I'm not convinced I need it," or "I would really rather wait until the next budget year," or "I think I can negotiate with you."

Isolating the objection will confirm or suspend your suspicions. Here's how it works: When faced with "You're too expensive," respond with: "Price aside, is there any other reason why you wouldn't go with our proposal?"

The "price aside" isolation is a way of asking the customer, "Is price the only thing that's in the way here?" If the answer is no, then price is the real and only objection, and the customer probably wants to negotiate. If the answer is yes, or if there is any hesitation in the customer's voice, keep digging. There are probably unresolved issues or objections (questions) that you need to get out on the table before an agreement can be reached.

Find the real concern by isolating the objection!

# 61. You Can Beat the Dreaded Objection

*"Your competition is offering the exact same package at a lower price."*

It's approaching the time to close the sale. Then the customer grows a bit quiet, looks you in the eye, and says, "But one of your competitors is offering their solution for $200 a month less! Why should we buy from you?"

I'm going to let you in on a little secret. When a customer throws that objection out on the table, there's a subtle translation going on:

The customer says: "You're the same as them, but they have a better price."

The customer means: "We want you to lower your price."

How do I know that? Well, for openers, if I were a customer and I really thought that your competition had a comparable product, at a lower price, I would just go ahead and buy from the competition! What would I have to gain by telling the losing sales rep the reasons for my decision *before* I made it? So, of course, if a customer does bother to tell you that they are going with someone else, especially if that conversation happens in a face-to-face meeting, then there is a very good chance that they want you to do something about it, which is lower your price or convince them that they should alter their course.

So here's the thing to do. Respond to this objection by asking, "If the prices were equal, who would you choose?" Obviously, there are only two answers to that question.

Answer #1: If they say, "We would choose you," then your follow-up question must be "Why?" Think about it. If the customer prefers you, there must be a reason. Therefore, your customer's answer to "Why?" is really your ammunition to justify a higher price tag. It is the extra value that you and your company bring to the table and, best of all, it's value defined in *your customer's own words*.

This is a tough dialog to have with a customer because they will always be concerned about price, especially if there is a competitor nearby, dangling a "similar" solution at a lower price. But fear not! You have one universal truth working in your favor, one that even penny-pinching customers have to admit—that nothing in this world is free. If there are reasons why they want to do business with you, then those reasons have a price tag. The more or better the reasons, the higher the price.

*Warning*: Resist the urge to explain! The discussion works when your customer is telling *you* the reasons. For the seller, there is a real temptation to jump in and explain to the customer why they should pay more. Don't waste your breath. Your customer must be the one who is doing the talking because value is only concrete when the customer is willing to pay for it. It's not easy, but be secure in the knowledge that most rational people will admit that they don't really expect to get something for nothing, and it is this basic premise that should allow you to win the business at a higher price.

A simple example is the value of a current relationship. I was selling to an existing customer who told me that she was going with the competition because their proposal substantially undercut my own. This financial decision was being made by someone who, while quite senior in the organization, had no idea of our current track record or relationship (she was the new CFO). In truth, we had been dealing with this company for the past several years and our track record was excellent.

It was up to me to take the initiative. I led a one-hour discussion about the true value of our current relationship and the risks associated with throwing all that away. As the customer answered my questions, she began to realize the true costs and risks associated with changing to a less expensive supplier, and then she wasn't so eager to make the switch. After doing a little of her own investigation, she was convinced and in the end they stayed with us, despite a significantly higher price.

Bottom line: If we hadn't had that discussion, I would have lost the business because my customer would never have thought to analyze the value of the current relationship. Remember, it's always easier for customers to justify picking the lowest bid ("I'm saving money") than justify paying more.

Now, as for Answer #2, if the customer says, *"If the price was the same we would still buy from your competitor,"* then feel free to start crying. But before you leave their office, find out why they are buying from your competitor, and then politely excuse yourself, and find a quiet corner in a coffee shop so you can re-read this book. Thank you.

If the customer wants to buy from you, find out why! It's the ammunition you need to justify a higher price!

# 62. Conditions Are Not Objections

*"It's got to be up and running by month-end! Can you do that?"*

Have you ever been hit by an objection that you could not overcome? Guess what? If you couldn't overcome it, then it probably wasn't an *objection*. Chances are it was a condition. A few chapters back, we reviewed the concept that objections are really just questions, albeit tough questions that often surface when you're trying to close the sale. Conditions are not questions, although they often masquerade as such; they're statements that you must accept.

Let me give you an example. Your customer says, "Your product is too expensive!" Is that an objection or a condition? The answer lies in the true meaning of the words. Is this person really averse to spending *x* dollars on the product (a statement of fact, and therefore a condition), or is it a lack of understanding as to what makes it worth the price (an objection). Making this distinction is important because it will change the way you respond to the customer.

If you accept the customer's statement as a condition (by definition, you must accept all conditions!), then you must move on to other products that are in your customer's price range. If you accept the customer's statement as an objection, then you must clarify the value of the product on the assumption that your customer will be convinced and buy from you.

It's tricky business. Let's try another example. You're a car dealer, and a customer says, "Your sports car does not have the acceleration that I need." Objection or condition? The answer? Well, if it's an objection, then you are assuming that either the customer is in error and the acceleration is better than they think, or that while the acceleration is less than excellent, the other features of the car make the poor acceleration an acceptable tradeoff. In the first case you would answer the objection by clarifying the true acceleration. In the second, you would accept the acceleration as a drawback, but strengthen the reasons for purchase with the other benefits of the car. In both cases you handled the statement as an objection. Why?

Because you "handled" it, which is where the term "handling objections" comes from. In other words, you answered the customer's question.

But what if it were a condition? What if, come hell or high water, your customer was not going to accept the engine's performance? Well, then, you would look pretty ridiculous trying to "handle" their condition as an objection. In fact, I have actually watched a car salesman argue with a customer who had a condition. This guy just didn't get it. (The customer eventually got fed up and left.) In this case, the right move is to accept the condition and either provide a better engine option or look at another car.

I hope you can see that a failure to differentiate between an objection and a condition can be disastrous. Therefore, I submit, once again, that the secret to conditions is to understand the true issue. Back to our car example. The high-performing salesperson would have asked: "What level of acceleration were you looking for?" Or "Where does acceleration rank on your shopping list?" Or "Do you have a minimum engine size or performance in mind?"

The next time you hit the stop sign, ask your customer to clarify their concern. You will know through their comments whether it is an objection (something you can handle) or a condition (something you must accept).

Here's a final thought on conditions that isn't exactly inspirational. You have probably lost, or will probably lose, a sale because of a condition. These kinds of conditions are often called "show stoppers." When you're about to close a deal, and you start to feel an objection coming from your customer, it's natural to tense up and fear the objection. In reality, it's not an objection that you fear. What you fear is a condition— a condition that you can't meet—a "show stopper."

I have only one truth on this one. Show stoppers are out there! There are customers that just won't buy your product or service because of something you have (a high price tag or a bad reputation) or something you lack (a certain feature they need). It's your job to determine early on in the selling process what and where are the show stoppers. You do that by asking questions early in the sale to make sure that you don't get zapped at the end. (Frankly, I would much rather tuck my tail between my legs on the first call than on the last.) One final thing: If you're going to face a condition at the end of the sale, *make sure it's a condition you can meet.*

# Part 14

# Commitments

# 63. Manage the "Close" Through Bite-Sized Commitments

*"I liked Kim's style. She was assertive without being pushy."*

Why do salespeople get so nervous when it's time to close the sale?

Well, that's kind of a no-brainer, isn't it? It's time to find out if your effort was all worth it! Will you get the ultimate reward or the ultimate rejection?

But why do we accept the end, or "close" as it is often referred to, as the time to find out if we win or lose? I must confess it's easy to do. I remember doing the same thing early in my sales career: hoping, waiting, wondering, as I got closer to the final close. But as I sit here today, I ask myself, "What was I thinking?" Why did I let the outcome of the sale remain a closely guarded secret until the bitter end? Surely there must be a way of getting commitment earlier in the sale, a way to lower my stress as I move down the "garden path" of the sales cycle.

There is. Consider the movie *What About Bob?* Bill Murray plays a psychiatric patient who has trouble coping with the enormity and complexity of life. Richard Dreyfuss plays his counselor. He treats Bob by getting him to look at his life as a series of small, manageable steps rather than a whole overwhelming journey. By creating baby steps or bite-sized goals, Bob is able to move ahead with his life with a sense of confidence and self-control.

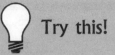 **Try this!**

Identify a sales opportunity for which you have a scheduled appointment. Before going on the call, determine what bite-sized commitment is required to move this opportunity closer to the sale. Now, put that into the form of a question to your customer—for example, "I would like to meet with you in two weeks to discuss the results of my investigation. Can we schedule a time now?"

Write down your question, somewhere at the top of your call plan or somewhere you will see it. At the end of the call, ask the commitment question!

A large and complex sale is a lot like life, in that both can seem overwhelming at times. So here's Bob's survival technique adapted to complex sales.

The bite-sized steps in the sale are equated to the commitments you gain throughout the selling process. If you manage the sale properly, obtaining the final commitment from the customer should not be as big a challenge. Final commitment should simply be the logical conclusion to all of the smaller commitments that you have been getting along the way.

Here's a game plan. At the beginning of each sales call, try to forecast the outcome of the call in terms of a small manageable goal that you want to reach. Ask yourself this question: "What level of commitment will I need at the end of this call in order to move the sales process forward?" (Do you want a second appointment? Do you want to arrange a demo? Do you want to get agreement that you should present a proposal?) With this in mind, at the end of the call put your assumptions aside, take a deep breath, and ask the commitment question. (Don't be shy here; be resolute!) Here are a few examples:

- What's the next step?
- Can we move forward with . . .?
- Would you agree that …?
- Are you ready to put the time and resources towards …?
- Is it time to look at a proposal?
- Does it make sense to arrange a demo?
- How committed are you at this point?
- Is there room in the budget this year?

Questions like this should be a mainstay of every call's wrap-up. There should be no doubt in either your mind or the customer's about where each of you stands every time you walk out of their office. I guarantee you that if you make a point of practicing the art of bite-sized steps, the final close will almost seem a little anticlimactic. Why?

*Because your customer will expect the question, and you will both know the answer.*

## IN REVIEW

Getting a commitment for the sale is easier if you have obtained smaller commitments all the way through the sale. You should strive to get a bite-sized commitment at the end of every call—a commitment to the next logical step in the sales process.

# 64. Mapping Isn't Easy— But It Will Save Your Sale

*"Before we move on, Jack, can you explain your decision-making process for me?"*

How many times have I lost a sale to a competitor I didn't even know existed?

How many times were decisions delayed because a committee had to review the proposal?

How many times did a customer look at me and say, "Looks good, but we're not ready to do it this year"?

All three examples were commonplace in my miserable existence until I embraced the *art of mapping.*

It is one tactical skill that has had a huge impact on my selling career, and it does not surprise me when I find that successful salespeople across a wide spectrum of industries are employing the same tactic.

The concept of mapping is a simple one. You are driving to a family get-together. You are at point A and wish to get to point B, but you don't know the way. Would you wing it? Would you drive down streets at random until you just happened to find your destination out of sheer luck? Of course not. You'd get a map.

We all know how complex decision processes are becoming these days. Often the customer's own organization is confused about the approval needed for any one particular sale. The decision map depicting point A as your initial call and point B as the signature on an order may be fraught with all kinds of detours, dead ends, and wrong turns if you make the journey without consulting a map.

That's what I did in each of the examples cited previously. I made the long and difficult sales journey without the aid of the customer's decision-making map, only to find that I had made a wrong turn somewhere along the way and become utterly lost.

It takes a little courage, but you can build on your commitment questions with the following mapping questions:

- Can you tell me how this decision will be made?
- What steps will you need to take?
- Who will be involved?
- Once you've reviewed the proposal, what happens next?
- What's the decision process here?
- How long will the process take?
- When would you like to have the final solution implemented?
- How long will it take you to review your options?
- What roadblocks could get in our way?
- What's your sense of urgency on this one?

The answers to those questions will formulate your map. As you get to every checkpoint along the way (each commitment step), pull the map back out and check with your existing or new contact.

- Am I still on track?
- Has the roadmap changed?
- Have there been any organizational changes that I should be aware of?
- Does it still look as if your final decision will be next month?

Here's an interesting benefit of mapping for you to consider. If you get a customer to outline their map and take ownership of the process,

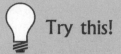 Try this!

Find a quiet conference room that contains a whiteboard. Now think about one of your larger and complex accounts, one where there is a current sales opportunity very early in its development.

On the top left of the whiteboard, write the letter "A" and beside it qualify where the sales decision sits today. For example, "Sheila is interested in looking at outsourcing alternatives."

On the bottom right of the white board, write the letter "B" and qualify the outcome of the sale: "Sheila's boss says yes to our outsourcing proposal."

Put a forecasted sale revenue amount and a forecasted date beside "B" (if possible).

Now comes the fun part. Draw in as many boxes as needed between "A" and "B," where a box is defined as a step in the customer's decision-making process. For example, "The manager needs to review the proposal. Jane, the marketing director, needs to give her input. The user group will test the solution first. And Sheila has to look at three quotes."

When you have finished, try to put the steps (boxes) in order and mark a completion date beside each box.

Okay, let's test your work.

- Question #1: Is there enough time to complete all of the steps and get to B by the date indicated on your map?
- Question #2: Are their any detours or problem areas between the boxes? In other words, do you need to do something during this journey to ensure that the map leads to your solution?
- Question #3: Do you need some more information? Are there empty boxes or unclear paths that need to be examined?

One of two things usually happen as a result of this exercise. First, you will get some ideas as to how you can influence the customer's decision map so that the sale goes to you instead of the competition. Second, you will realize that your map needs work, and it's time to go and talk to your customer.

doesn't that take the pressure off your final close? There should be no surprise, right? After all, the decision to buy your solution is located right there on the map!

When you're on a long and difficult sales journey, use your customer's map to get there!

## IN REVIEW

Mapping is a metaphor for the decision-making journey. The map identifies all of the stops, turns, and detours that a buying organization has to make before it can say yes to your proposal. Without the map, you and your customer can get lost in the many policies, procedures, and people that influence the sale along its decision journey.

Don't get lost in the decision jungle. With your customer's help, take the time to create the map and then follow it.

# 65. Sales Don't Advance on Their Own

*"I was impressed by how Roz finished each call with a summary and 'next steps' and started each call with a recap and agenda. He kept us on track and moving along."*

While bite-sized commitments and mapping are essential to the selling process, neither works very well unless you are constantly moving towards an objective. And it's you who moves things forward. It's as simple as that.

We have a significant selling truth here. The salesperson alone has the responsibility for keeping things going! Thus, the idea of sales advances. This is more a state of mind than a skill, or at least I like to think of it in those terms.

Let me set this up properly. How many times have you left a customer's office without any real commitment or agreement to move forward? Perhaps you felt it was inappropriate because your relationship was so good that moving forward was a basic and mutual assumption. Or maybe the call was running late, so everyone scrambled for their empty coffee cups and left the meeting nodding a familiar *"I'll call you."*

To avoid those ambiguous endings, I learned to create a state of mind that was summoned when a sales call was ending. I call it the

"Who's got the ball on this?" mindset. It's a question that now pops up in my head instinctively as a meeting or telephone call comes to a close.

If your customer has the ball—meaning that the next step is in their court and not yours—you have lost control of the sale. You cannot possibly get that bite-sized commitment and continue the journey on their decision map because the impetus to do so rests with your customer, not with you. Here's an example. If your customer says, "I'll get back to you," then no agreement or commitment has been reached and the ball is not in your court.

A symptom of this disease is the propensity for low-performing sales reps to have an empty calendar at the beginning of their week. If there are no appointments or telephone calls set up, it's clear to me that the ball is not in their court. They are reduced to a career of waiting and reacting, which is at best nerve-wracking, and at the very least a waste of valuable time and energy.

Get this message into your subconscious:

*I must have the ball at the end of every call.*

*I must have the ball at the end of every call.*

*I must have the ball at the end of every call.*

*There's no place like home, there's no ... (Sorry about that!)*

Example #1: As your sales call to review the initial proposal draws to a close, think about the next logical step. As you summarize, the customer takes control by saying: "I'll have to talk to my manager and see what he thinks of your proposal." In response, do not say: "Okay. Well good luck and have a nice day."

What you should say is, "That's great! Why don't we meet at the end of the week and see how you made out," or "Why don't you let me get a copy of the proposal to her and I will call to get her input," or "I'll call you first thing Friday morning—say at 7:30—so that we can make changes to the proposal on the basis of her review." Congratulations! You're in control. There's a commitment to a next step, and the sales cycle is advanced.

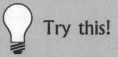 **Try this!**

Open up your day planner to next week. How many scheduled activities are there?

Now, open up your forecasted sales for the current month
or quarter. How many of those sales are in your control? How
many balls are in your customers' courts?

The answers to the questions will either make you smile
with satisfaction or give you something to do!

Example #2: Your customer says, "I'll have to get back to you with
those figures next week." How easy it would be to say, "Okay, I'll look
forward to your call"! Fortunately, because your subconscious is shout-
ing out the orders (Get the ball! Get the ball!), you say, "Great! Why
don't you fax them on Tuesday and let's put aside 15 minutes—say at
4:30 at the end of the day—to review the figures and consider next
steps. I'll call you then." You're good!

If you want to lower your stress and shorten your sales cycles,
keep the ball in your court!

## In review

The easiest way to assess the amount of control that you have over
your sales cycles is to figure out "who has the ball." If the next step in
the cycle is in the hands of your customer, your customer has the ball. If
the next step resides with you, the ball is in your court and that means
you have control.

# 66. Hard Closers Tend to Burn Bridges

*"I hammered the hell out of him! He was practically shaking when he signed the deal!"*

There are legendary salespeople in every industry. And many of those legends stem from the same sales skill—the skill of closing. One of my favorites is the story about a salesperson who was notorious for his aggressive "hard" closes. I call it the legend of the "pen close" and it goes something like this:

He would appear at the customer's door unannounced and quickly produce a completed sales contract and a gold pen, dropping both on his customer's desk for maximum "shock value." Each time the customer would object to the sale, he would pick up the pen and place it down closer to the spot that required a signature. His menacing demeanor combined with his constant assurances "would I ever steer you wrong?" eventually would overcome the weary customer. Within five or ten minutes of his arrival, the salesperson would pocket the signed contract, claim yet another victory, and head off to a dry martini and a big steak lunch.

What I enjoy most about this story is that it completely and unabashedly flies in the face of what successful salespeople are really doing these days. This guy didn't "sell" his customer, and he certainly didn't build a relationship. The whole story boils down to how you can get a quick and easy sale by bullying your customers!

Could such a story really have happened? Well, yes and no. The tale itself is mostly fiction—a good story that got better over the years of retelling. However, pressure techniques were definitely in vogue in years past, and legends abound about salespeople who have used such techniques to close a sale. Which begs the question: why would any customer bow to that kind of pressure?

Customers say "yes" under pressure when certain circumstances apply:

1. I don't have much choice.
2. I don't have much risk (i.e., low-value decision with minimal impact on my operation).
3. I'm unaware of the risks (i.e., the facts as presented, seem okay to me).

But today's customers have lots of options! And wait! That's not all! They're also more educated. They're also more accountable for their decisions. They also have limited operating budgets. They also make "strategic" decisions that affect the whole organization versus just a few people. To sum up, they've got choices, they've got smarts, and they've got more risk involved in their decisions! How far do you think our legendary "pen close" would get, operating in today's corporate buying and selling environment?

Not far, although despite the change of times, there are those who still employ pressure tactics today. In my experience, pressure techniques are used because the salesperson is using force to try to compensate for the fact that the customer is not ready to reach an agreement. If you force it down their throats, watch out! There are bound to be repercussions from the reasons behind their resistance in the first place.

Closing *should* be relatively easy. Yes, you still have to ask the tough question. It's your job to close the sale. But the answer to that question should be the natural and predictable conclusion of a sale because you have handled all of the issues and discussed all of the risks.

*Good closers are assertive, without being aggressive. Good closers close once. It's all they ever need.*

Look at it another way. If you work your heart out trying to establish a strong relationship with your customer, aren't they going to look at you funny when you put on a hard closing schtick? They're going to wonder if you really cared about their issues in the first place, seeing as how you want to rush to the "signing" so quickly.

Don't burn your bridges by trying to force a short-term win through a hard close. Find out why there is resistance, commit to fixing it, and then go back to close the sale. When you think about getting aggressive the next time, remember the story of the "pen close," and imagine that you are the customer on the other side of that desk. As the proverbial pen is dropped in front of you, ask yourself the same question that your customers ask each and every time they prepare to make the final decision: *Are the risks of this sale outweighed by the benefits it will provide?*

# Part 15

# Negotiating

# 67. Negotiating and Selling Are Not the Same Things

*"How low can you go?"*

In my second year at Xerox, I took on a new account right in the middle of a big sale. I can recall being surprised by how easy it was to get the customer's agreement to go with Xerox instead of the competition. This customer hardly knew me, and yet here he was about to sign a $50,000 equipment lease, within a week of our introduction—or so I thought.

Despite his assurances, and my bold claims of victory, getting the agreement signed was an entirely different story. It all began with a distinct change in his tone when I produced the paperwork for his signature. He looked up at me and said, "Not just yet." I felt a big "Uh-oh!" rising in my throat as he rolled up his sleeves and began to take my sales agreement apart, page by page.

And so began a process of negotiation that lasted six months! Yes, I did get the sale, but it almost killed me! And I can tell you now, that a second look at the final sales agreement would tell you that I definitely got less than I bargained for (probably much to the delight of the customer!).

Here's a brief recap: four days of selling; 180 days of negotiating. What a ride!

It was fun. It was exhausting. It was intense. It was frustrating. It was annoying. And all rolled into one, it was a valuable experience for me. When I finally walked back to the office with his signature, I remember thinking, "Thank God, that's over! I'll never do that again!"

But as it turned out, I was wrong. Lengthy negotiations were commonplace, especially in the early years of my career. I seemed to spend a lot of time and energy negotiating to get the "final" signature, long after the "sale" itself was over. Why did that happen? It happened because I thought that negotiating and selling were the same thing. They're not! So let's explore the differences.

Selling is *getting agreement*. You "sell" a customer on the need for your goods and services. Negotiating is *coming to terms*. Negotiation becomes necessary when two parties agree on the goods and services for exchange, but can't quite agree on all of the finer details. It's the process of give and take.

The confusion over the terms begins with a common misperception that negotiating is an important part of selling. Yes, negotiating is important. No, it's not part of selling. Separating the two is crucial. If you believe that negotiating is part of selling, then nothing is stopping you from negotiating during the selling process, or in other words, negotiating before an agreement has been reached. So, here's a question: If there's no agreement, then what are you negotiating? Why would any customer "give" in the negotiation process if they weren't convinced that they needed your goods and services in the first place?

The solution? *Finish selling before you negotiate*, or suffer the consequences! Let's look back at my example. That difficult six-month period might have involved many different things, but negotiation wasn't one of them. I know that now, because in hindsight I had no agreement during that time. The customer did not really want or need our solution and, therefore, negotiation could not take place. Yes, he "preferred" Xerox to the competition—he told me that! But he wasn't sold on us. He didn't really need us. There was no true sales agreement. (Come to think of it, how could I expect to sell him after only four days on the job?) Consequently, he was quite content to let our meetings and telephone conversations drag on and on. And worse, those six months weren't about give and take. Without really being sold, my customer had no incentive to "give." Therefore, he did all of the taking, and I did all of the giving. I wanted that sale, and he knew it.

I negotiated before I finished selling, and it's a very common mistake. Witness those around you who seem to spend a lot more time negotiating than they do selling. Aren't those the same people who are the first to complain about price increases? I have found that many of those complainers suffer from the same malady—they're lazy sellers. They try to negotiate their way out of a bad selling job because lowering your price is a lot easier and faster than building value (selling) to justify a higher price. I guess if you're the lowest game in town, that's okay. But with the amount of competition out there today, there is a good chance that you are not the cheapest, and that means you will lose to someone who can go lower than you can. A good rule of thumb here is *negotiate after you've sold the customer on your solution.*

And how do you know that the customer is sold? Why, you ask them, of course: "Before we talk about the price, let me ask you a question: Do you really believe that this is the right solution for you?" If they say "Yes," then you have the leverage that you will need to negotiate successfully. Quite simply, negotiating leverage is based on the fact that they want what you have (the solution); conversely, you want what they have (the money). At that crucial point the negotiation can begin.

The really tricky part of this lesson is having the guts to ask the tough question, as opposed to assuming that the customer is sold. Avoiding the tough question can be doubly disastrous, as I learned in yet another case in the Xerox school of hard knocks. On this occasion, my negotiating efforts were doomed from the beginning, because the customer had no intention of buying from Xerox. Of course, I just assumed that the customer was sold on us and proceeded to waste the better part of two weeks haggling over the equipment price. In reality the customer was negotiating with us in order to drive a competitor's price down— and the competitor eventually got the sale.

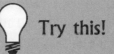
**Try this!**

If and when you get into the middle of a negotiation where you feel that the customer is all "take" and no "give," take a break from the negotiation and ask your customer an important "selling" question: "Are we in agreement that this is the right solution for your needs?"

If the answer is yes, then proceed with the give and take. If the answer is no, then stop negotiating and go back to selling.

Negotiate with the customer after they have said yes to your solution.

## IN REVIEW

Negotiation is the art of coming to terms (give and take) once the seller and customer have agreed upon the products and services (the "solution"). Negotiating before an agreement is reached is putting the cart before the horse, and it gives the customer a distinct negotiating advantage because if your customer doesn't need "it" (no agreement), then why would they "give" anything to you? Customers who don't need you will do all of the "taking" and none of the "giving."

## RECOMMENDED READING

While there are lots of good negotiating books out there, I particularly like Neil Rackham's offering, *Major Account Sales Strategy* (New York: McGraw-Hill, 1989). It's a very thought-provoking review of negotiating and a must on any corporate seller's bookshelf.

# 68. When Negotiating, Remember the Golden Rules

*"I knew that they would be looking at competition, so I had to give them our best price up front!"*

As you prepare to negotiate, keep the following five Golden Rules in mind:

1. **Build a strong relationship.** When you get to the negotiation stage you want to be working *with* your customers, not *against* them. Avoid the cloak-and-dagger that accompanies a low-trust negotiation.

2. **Negotiate late.** What's the most common mistake committed by inexperienced sales reps? *Too much, too soon* (Huthwaite's Major Account Sales Strategy). Do yourself a favor and get commitment on your solution first! Negotiation is really about coming to terms, and that should happen only at the end of the sale—when the selling is done.

3. **Know your range.** If you get face to face with a client who is looking for some realistic concessions, know what you can—and can't—give away. If you're forced to stop the negotiation and go back to the office (for example, to check with a manager or consult your pricing sheets), you may give your competitor the window of opportunity that they've been waiting for.

4. **If you're going to give something away, make sure you get something in return.** Negotiating is about give and take. If you make it a "give" only, your customers will

assume that, since you're so generous, you must possess a gift that "keeps on giving"! Watch out! Your customers will drag out the negotiation process until they are sure you have nothing left to give. Getting something in return is your way of telling customers that negotiating is about *tradeoffs*, not gift-giving. It also signals the customers that you are already at the bottom of the negotiating barrel; that is, since your proposal is fat-free, you will require some kind of return for what you are prepared to give away.

5. **Be prepared to walk away from the sale.** Customers know when their sellers are desperate. If they perceive this is true of you—if they know you will continue to negotiate and not walk away—then they will continue to negotiate for as long as possible and squeeze every last concession out of you. Prepare yourself mentally: Be able to walk from the sale—at least temporarily—when your customer asks for more than you are prepared to give. Being able to draw a line in the sand will help both you and your customer recognize when the negotiation is over.

# 69. Everybody Wants a "Good Deal"

*"I was going to wait until next year, but they put a really nice package together and I couldn't say no."*

Remember this Marxian saying from political science class: "From each according to his ability, to each according to his need"?

I remember Marx's words well, but the world just doesn't work that way! Every customer wants special treatment and no one wants to end up with the short end of the stick, especially when it comes to making a deal. It's as natural as the day is long. Even the "nicest" customers want to feel special, that somehow they got the best deal in town!

Everybody wants a good deal—so give it to them. This doesn't mean that you should lower your price (that seems to be the standard sales' knee-jerk reaction when customers say they want a good deal). Instead, create a unique or custom solution that effectively gives your customer what you want them to have, but the way *they* want it. Don't forget that everyone's different; different people have different ideas of what a "good deal" means, and that's okay. Figure out what is valuable to your client (through questions, of course) and then position yourself, your product, and your company to deliver on that value.

Perhaps your customer's idea of value is getting the lowest price possible. Then it's your job to make it clear that you are delivering the best price available. Document each and every price concession in your proposal, and clearly show all hard-dollar discounts. Next, attach a price tag to any feature or service of value to the customer. For example, if your customer likes the "help desk" service as outlined in your proposal (that is, a 1-800 line for 24-hour support), then don't just list it as part of the whole package. That's a waste. The only way that the customer will value the help desk is to understand the cost associated with it. So outline that cost in your proposal.

*Everything of value has a price.*

On the other hand, maybe your customer's idea of a "good deal" is getting some "extras" thrown in for free. Forget about it. Nothing is free. Don't trivialize something that you are going to include by "throwing it in" for nothing. That's like saying, *"We were going to throw that component in anyway, so you can have it!"* It's your job to document everything that you offer the customer as part of the "deal," and then document the impact that each item will have on the customer. Finally, it's also your job to tally up the price of each and every extra, so that the customer knows it cost you something to give it away.

Everybody wins when you give a customer the "value" of a lifetime. If they want to call it a "deal," then that's just fine.

# Part 16

# Competition

# 70. Lock Your Competition Out Before Writing Your Proposal

*"Not only did we have the same solution, but we also came in at almost 20 percent less than everyone else. How did we lose that deal?"*

A "lockout" is something you can do and your competition can't. You "lock" your competition "out" of the sale. Understanding and leveraging your lockouts will help keep your competition away from a sale. And the lockout strategy is one you will need to employ before setting foot in a customer's office. Here's the reason: *If you sell generic solutions to meet generic needs, some competitor will always come along with a better price—and then you're dead!*

Here's an example from personal experience. On one occasion I took an existing customer who had no urge to buy, and did a first-rate job at identifying and exploring the need for a new photocopier. At the end of the selling cycle, he thanked me for my diligent investigation work, and then promptly bought from the competition. In my shock and amazement, I was half expecting to get a flower arrangement from my competitor because I did all of the ground work for *him*! Hell, if it wasn't for me, the customer would have stuck with his current equipment!

Unfortunately, my competitor's photocopier could do everything that was needed, but cost about 15 percent less. I didn't understand or identify the customer's need for my photocopier specifically. I did not develop a need for my "lockouts." It was a bitter pill to swallow. So, if you don't want to hand a sale over to a competitor on a silver platter, take heed of this advice:

*Lock your competition out early in the sale by identifying and investigating those problems that you can fix better than they can.*

Lockouts can be a variety of things. Obviously, if you have a specific feature that is unique, you should be looking for problems in your customer's operation that your feature can fix. However, lockouts can be linked to a lot more than just features (which is important if you are in a commodity marketplace, where all the features tend to look the same). For example, I locked out a competitor on the basis of my company's existing relationship with the customer. In that case, our competitive strength was our longstanding history of quality service, a service that the customer did not want to risk losing. In essence, we locked our competitors out, because we were *there*, and they weren't. Other examples of lockouts include flexibility, customization, service effectiveness and response, scalability, leading-edge technology, regional representation, and strategic partnerships—and the list goes on and on.

Here's a word of caution about the lockout strategy that relates to Chapter 74 in this book, "Perception Is Reality." In my previously discussed service example, our ability to win the business, on the basis of our current customer relationship, was due to the customer's perception that current service levels were very important. Unfortunately for me, I have also lost business because, all other things being equal, the customer wanted to try somebody new. In that case, our current service level actually worked against us, despite the fact that the service was excellent.

Another common perception issue concerns leading-edge technology. It may be a lockout for those customers who want the latest and greatest, but it may also be a distinct disadvantage for those customers who like to avoid the "bleeding edge" and always opt for the "tried and true."

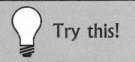 **Try this!**

1. Work with your sales team to identify your "lockouts." Determine those characteristics of your solution, or organization, that are unique to you, or at least form a very strong competitive advantage.

2. Develop a questioning strategy that helps you uncover business problems that your lockouts fix.

3. When the customer is ready for a recommendation (a proposal), stop! It's time to do a little test. Ask your customer to create a shopping list—a list of the things they want and that you will address in your proposal. If you've done a good sales job, your lockouts will be on that list, somewhere near the top, you hope. If none of your lockouts are on their shopping list, you are in danger of losing the sale to a lower-cost competitor. I suggest that you put the brakes on and go back to "selling" before they begin shopping!

4. Let your customers shop, but be sure to keep in touch with them (see Chapter 71, "'Bookending' Will Improve Your Odds"). As long as the customer continues to use their shopping list as a guide, you should win against the competition.

*Customers are people, and different people value different lockouts.* Therefore, lockouts are situation- and customer-specific, and can change dramatically between different organizations and different types of people within the same organization. You will have to find out which lockout applies the same way that you have to find out everything else; in other words, you have to "sell" your lockouts.

One thing is for sure. You will feel much better about the outcome of a sale if the person making the decision knows that you can satisfy their shopping list better than the competition. Better yet, think about your negotiating power when you know that there is something on your customer's shopping list that *only you* can satisfy. Believe me, it feels good!

For every sale, there is always a low-cost competitor. *Lock them out!*

## IN REVIEW

Lock your competition out early in the sale, by developing needs that you are better positioned to meet.

# 71. Bookending Will Improve Your Odds

*"Your proposal looks good, but we're going to have to look at a few of your competitors."*

Most customers shop around. It helps them get educated, it keeps their suppliers honest, and it lets them explore different ways to solve their problems.

The irony is that most customers would probably choose not to shop around *if* they had *one supplier* who could educate them, was consistently honest, and objectively explored all options. But is that likely? The truth is, we salespeople are usually pushing one solution—ours! Since that's not a secret to our customers, it only makes sense that they would venture out into the world to see how different vendors would approach their problem, so that they can choose the solution that makes the most sense for them.

Unfortunately, the customer's shopping exercise can be a stressful time for us salespeople. As we sit idly by, our customers are consorting with the enemy. And, no doubt, the enemy is going to sway them away from our solution, opting for some other means to solve the customer's problem. What can you do about it? How can you get control of the situation and back in front of your customer? Permit me to introduce the skill of "bookending."

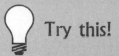 Try this!

Scenario #1: If you help to establish your customer's needs, you are in the driver's seat. It should be relatively easy to position yourself first and last. If you have done the work to set the bar, you should have the relationship that will allow you to take more control. Make sure you get an idea of the number of competitors and the length of time it will take to complete the shopping process.

Scenario #2: If you get a call from a customer looking for a quote, chances are you are just one stop on their shopping rounds and someone else has had the opportunity to bid first. That puts you at a disadvantage because you have not had a chance to position your lockouts, and presumably someone else has! If you respond to the bid "as is," you will probably lose, especially if the bar is set correctly (you will get locked out by someone else). Therefore, you will have to do one of two things:

1. Get back in and reestablish the needs (reset the bar and change the customer's shopping list).
2. Ask to be the last competitor on the shopping rounds so that you can position yourself against the entire field at that time.

Either way, bookending establishes an important fact: If you are not first in, you are at a distinct disadvantage. Don't give up, but don't underestimate your competitor's lockouts. Get in there and sell!

To begin with, we know that there are two bookends on a shelf. The length of the shelf is a metaphor for the length of time in a sales cycle. The bookend on the left is the first stop on the customer's shopping rounds. You want to be that bookend on the left in that you want to have your proposal in the customer's hands first because it's your chance to "set the bar" against which your competitors will be measured. If you have done a good job of investigating the customer's needs, you will set the bar with a proposal that meets those needs better than anyone else can (see Chapter 70, "Lock Your Competition Out Before Writing Your Proposal"). In other words, your activities before the shopping phase are centered on setting the bar beyond your competitor's reach.

But don't stop there. Sometimes you think you've got it made, only to find out that the customer, on their third stop on their shopping rounds, was offered a "great deal" and that's where the process stopped, in consequence freezing you out. It seems that the customer forgot all of the really good reasons to buy from you, and was enticed by a good price. Thus, in the spirit of bookending, get a commitment from your customer to revisit your proposal after all of the proposals have been submitted. That's the period of time at the end of the customer's shopping phase, the bookend on the right side of the shelf. You can easily justify your reason for revisiting your customer. It is only fair that, if questions or new needs surface during the process of shopping, you be given the opportunity to change your proposal accordingly (the "apples-to-apples comparison" idea).

Asking for bookends—that is, the right to propose first and revisit last—is not just good selling, but it's also a good test of your relationship. If your customer objects to your involvement, you may have overestimated the strength of your relationship. If it's solid, chances are the customer won't mind a telephone call at the end of the process. Better still, if they know you're coming back, and they've agreed to that, they should hesitate before making a price-motivated decision at door #3.

To sum up, be first in with your customer to set the bar, keep in contact throughout the process, and be there at the end to review. Your "bookend" control of their shopping process is a key to success.

Oh yes, one last thing on bookending, which comes from the study of human physiology: Scientists who study memory loss and retention have found that we tend to remember the first and last numbers in a sequence far more easily than numbers in the middle. So don't be a number in the middle! *Set the bar first and revisit last!*

## In Review

Bookending is always a good idea when it comes to your customer's shopping process. Be the bookend on the left to develop the needs and set the bar (with your lockouts). Be the bookend on the right to ensure that you revisit the process and address issues that your competitors have drummed up.

# 72. Beware of the Consultant

*"We spent six months helping them build the RFP and they turned around and bought from someone else!"*

I remember a selling situation that was particularly nasty. It was in the complex world of information technology (IT), where often customers will hire IT consultants to help them make significant hardware and software decisions. In this case, the consultant did not know as much about his customer's IT issues as he would have liked, so he made appointments with IT suppliers to become better educated. He then asked the suppliers to provide him with proposals in response to his client's IT problems. Sounds harmless enough, doesn't it?

Alas, this consultant took the knowledge that he had collected from one proposal in particular and then, in his presentation to the client, passed it off as his own. Are you getting the picture?

Watch out. If you run into a consultant who seems eager to pick your brain, do a little digging. Make sure that they are not just going to use your expertise and then dump you and your organization, long before you reach the person who's buying.

My suggestion when it comes to consultants is a simple one. Don't treat them like decision-makers, even though some will tell you that they are. Consultants are decision catalysts to be reckoned with (they take away some of your control). Get to know them, but get to know your other catalysts at the same time. No law says you must deal exclusively with the consultants—at least not in my book. Make sure you position your company with the consultants, as you would with other contacts in the account. In other words, find a way to make them win!

Just remember one thing: You will need to reach the real decision-maker or you may find that the consultant will lock you out of the sale.

*Don't underestimate the power of the consultant.*

Part  17

Unavoidable
Truths

# 73. Nothing Comes Before the Customer

*"Did you get that message about our team meeting next week? This will be the third time that I've rescheduled that demo."*

I was shocked recently when a relatively sane individual canceled a call on a major account—a sales call—because she was getting behind on her paperwork. ARGHHHHHH!

Which skill do you think advances a sale and results in revenue and profit for your company? (That's the stuff by which you are measured, bonused, promoted, and perhaps even fired.) Is it talking to customers about their business needs or opening mail? (Please don't feel compelled to answer that!) Okay, I know that the internal demands on salespeople can be daunting, but surely this is a case of mistaken priorities.

I think the answer is priority management and good old-fashioned stick-to-it-iveness (see Chapter 25, "Smarter Is Better than Harder."). Put a little time away every day (before or after business hours) to deal with the internal "junk," as I call it, and then stick to those times. If the hour that you set aside comes and goes, and you see no light at the end of the "junk" tunnel—TOO BAD. The junk can wait! Besides, if that salesperson gets to the end of the year and misses her sales quota, I'm quite sure that the vice-president of sales is not going to say, *"Well, you may have completely missed your sales target, but I must say, you do a bang-up job on paperwork. Keep up the good work, Ms. Jenkins!"*

The other big point here (which seems as plain as the nose on my face) is that customers are the number-one priority, and everything else ties for a distant second. If someone wants you to cancel your appointment with a customer because of internal meetings and such, perhaps you should ask the offending party to clear it with the vice-president of your sales organization first. I'm sure that your vice-president would be happy to explain why sales are more important than slide presentations (that was tongue in cheek, if you missed it!).

*The customer always comes first—still!*

# 74. Perception Is Reality

*"I just don't get it! It was one of the best demonstrations I've ever done, and they all just stood there with blanks on their faces..."*

When we visit our accounts as trained sales professionals, we often know more about certain business issues than our customers do. We become specialists, if you will, in the areas that are touched by our products and services. It would only stand to reason, then, that what may seem obvious to us experts may be much less obvious to everyone else.

Unfortunately, we're not doing the buying—we're doing the selling. Therefore, our view of reality is only important when it is shared by our customers.

In other words, our perception of reality isn't that important.

It's a nasty problem, this perception stuff, because there's often a gap between our view of reality and the customer's and it's hard to see. It lies beneath the surface of our conversations and meetings, until it comes out and "gets you" without warning. Hidden perceptions are like the submerged iceberg that poked at *Titanic*'s side and eventually sank her.

Here's an example.

I was once selling a large photocopier that derived much of its longevity and reliability from its size and strength. I had spent a considerable amount of time investigating each feature that contributed to its formidable competitive advantages of reliability and longevity. But much to *my* surprise, my impressive presentation, based on my perception of size, fell on deaf ears. The customer was completely unreceptive and actually got a little hostile as the presentation went on.

Why? Simple. His view of size and strength was the opposite of my own and I had failed to get his perception to the surface where I could see it, and thus manage it. So, if anything, I did more harm than good by emphasizing the size of the machine. His perception was that size was bad. He believed that "big" meant clumsy and obsolete.

I didn't agree with his perception, but it was *his* perception and at that point in the sale there was just no changing it.

The truth about size is irrelevant here. Size is good or size is bad … who cares? If, at the end of the day, "small is good" as far as the customer is concerned, then small *is* good. Period. In my case, I failed to identify his perception and the sale went to a smaller competitor.

One caveat: You don't necessarily have to accept a customer's perception. The fact is, the unit I was selling was at the top of its class in reliability and longevity due, in no small part, to its size and construction. Therefore, feel free to bring perceptions to the surface where you can see them, and then you can use your selling skills to change the customer's view.

Don't be another *Titanic*: Bring perceptions to the surface and either accept them—and change your course—or change them, and sink the iceberg before it sinks you!

Your customer's perception is *the only one* that matters.

# 75. If You Sweat the Uncontrollables, You're Dead

*"If that phone doesn't ring in the next half-hour, I'm going to jump out the window!"*

There is one sales skill that gets very little attention, and yet without it you're in serious trouble. It's the skill of not stressing over "uncontrollables" (those things in life over which you have little or no control). It's the "water off a duck's back" capability, and how you effectively deploy it is a matter of attitude.

I have run across a few salespeople who couldn't exercise the skill. The outcome was as predictable as it was disastrous. One fellow in particular comes to mind. He was a young and promising salesman when I met him, but it wasn't long before his stress level went through the roof. He just couldn't deal with "uncontrollables," and invariably his results went right down the tubes along with his health and personal life. He didn't last long at the company and I'm not sure what happened to him after that.

This situation did not have to happen. He was a good guy and a talented salesperson, but he never let anything roll off his back, no matter how uncontrollable it was. Every little thing seemed to eat away at him. Now, you might be saying, "That guy was a loser. I'd never let that happen to me!" Well, I'm not so sure about that. Let's examine the uncontrollables that were coming at him as a professional sales rep.

On the inside he had constant changes to his products and services, changes to the reporting structure, changes to his sales territory, monthly updates to his price list, quarterly and monthly changes to his goals and objectives (always getting tougher!), and constant changes to his time-management format, to his support staff, to his company's policies and procedures, to his manager's mood, and on and on. But the fun didn't stop there. Let's bring on the outside uncontrollables—changes to customers' decision-making processes, new competitors, service issues, meeting delays, road construction, bad weather, etc.

The rep would come back to the office each day wearing a look of defeat. It was all too much for him. Can you relate? (I know I can!) There are days when I have felt that way. But there are those around us who face the same mountain of uncontrollables without so much as a frown. How do they do it?

Well, here's a silly but fun suggestion that I picked up from one very successful salesperson who seemed to be the most relaxed individual on the planet. Now this idea may actually seem a little childish, but I can tell you that more than a few people have tried it and it seems to have helped. Here goes.

Create a little button or sticker that can be placed in a familiar place. It will say, "If you can't control it, forget it!" Now, the button in itself is just a gimmick (and not even an original one). The trick is in putting it in a place where you can see it often. It becomes a constant reminder. Put it in your daily planner or by your telephone, or next to your goals and objectives. Put it anywhere, as long as you can see it all the time. Sooner or later you will tune it out and at that point it will have outlived its usefulness. But for a while, it will remind you that life is short, so it's wise to stick to the stuff that you can control!

Control your stress by mentally letting go of the stuff you can't control!

A final word. As I'm sure you're aware, there is a lot more to this subject than creating a button. Your ability to "roll with the punches" is very much a function of your true colors, a.k.a. your compass (see

Chapter 77, "The World Will Always Be Changing"). If you're the kind of person who needs to have a lot of control, no button or other gimmick is going to take away your stress. Therefore, a word of advice to you control freaks: Stay out of corporate sales! You'll be miserable!

For everyone else, there is an old saying that summarizes this chapter nicely: "God grant me the serenity to accept the things I cannot change, courage to change the things I can, and the wisdom to know the difference."

# 76. Having All Your Eggs in One Basket Is Bad Business

*"It all comes down to one deal. Win it, and you're a hero; lose it and you're a zero!"*

Almost every seasoned salesperson will offer a weak smile in recognition of the "eggs in one basket" phenomenon. Many will wince at the painful memory of a time when their basket broke. The eggs-in-one-basket metaphor is usually associated with sales reps who bank on a single sale. If the sale is made, celebration. If the sale is lost, the end of the world. The emotion is particularly intense at the end of a quarter or year when some reps rest all of their bonus and commission hopes on a single sale.

With all eyes on the one basket, a not-so-funny thing happens. For openers, you start to lose the hunting/farming balance that assures consistent results. In fact, you tend to engage only in those activities that keep you close to your phone, or near the customer's office, in case they happen to call you in for the big finale. (I remember a time when I literally checked my voice mail every five minutes during a four-hour period.) Sometimes this singular focus can lead to a kind of myopic paralysis. In other words, you are counting on the deal so much, you can't think about anything else. (I have also caught myself sitting and staring at the phone for an entire day, just waiting

# Try this!

We are going to do a little exercise in "sales banks." A sales bank (or prospect bank) is a list of all of the sales opportunities that you are presently working on.

1. To begin, put the following headings across the top of your bank:
   - CUSTOMER
   - OPPORTUNITY
   - TOTAL VALUE
   - % CLOSE
   - ADJUSTMENT VALUE

2. Write down all of the customers' names (current sales opportunities) under the heading CUSTOMER.

3. For each CUSTOMER name in your bank, you should be able to identify the OPPORTUNITY (the products or services you are selling) and the TOTAL VALUE (the dollar amount or revenue stream associated with those products or services).

4. With the first three columns completed, scan your list. Are there any opportunities in your bank that are on shaky ground? For the purpose of this exercise, "shaky" means that while it looks like a great opportunity, the customer is really not serious about making a change yet. In other words, the customer is not committed to buying (write the word "shaky" beside the customer's name).

5. Add up the dollars in your TOTAL VALUE column to determine your grand total for all potential sales. Circle this figure at the bottom of the bank.

6. It's now time to analyze the eggs in your basket. We are going to put a "closing percentage" beside each of your opportunities. A closing percentage is a measure of the likelihood that the sale will go in your favor (versus being stalled or going to the competition). Here's the way to do it;

under the % CLOSE column, write down one of the following percentages:

- 10% for those customers who are not committed to buying (the "shaky" ones we talked about who really shouldn't be on your list in the first place);
- 15% for those customers who are buying, but prefer the competition;
- 25% for those customers that are buying, but have no preference for any one supplier;
- 50% for those customers who are buying and prefer your solution over the competition;
- 75% for those customers who are buying, prefer your solution and are working out the details of the sale with you.

7. When you have completed your percentage work, multiply the values in the two columns TOTAL VALUE and % CLOSE [$50,000 X 50% (.5) = $25,000]. Put this new revenue number under the heading ADJUSTMENT VALUE.

8. Add up the dollars in the ADJUSTMENT VALUE column to determine your grand total for all potential sales, adjusted by the likelihood that they will close. Circle it at the bottom of your bank.

9. Take a look at the two numbers circled at the bottom of your bank (TOTAL and ADJUSTMENT VALUE). How close are the numbers? How are you feeling right now?

10. One last step. Compare your ADJUSTMENT VALUE to your sales objective. How do the numbers compare? For example, if your monthly or quarterly objective is $100,000, do you have $100,000 or a greater number circled at the bottom of your bank in the ADJUSTMENT VALUE column?

11. What you have just completed is a quick but accurate analysis of the size and strength of your basket, and the number of cracks in your eggs. How do you feel about your basket? Is it time to go get some more eggs?

for something to happen. This is not fun, especially when the phone doesn't ring.) In this advanced stage of the disease, you carry your basket paralysis into your personal life. You try a walk in the park, or a quiet Sunday coffee, or even a long drive in the country—anything that might free you from your obsession: *"I need this deal. Everything is riding on it!"*

Of course, the more you obsess, the less likely you are going to get the deal done. Obsessive behaviors are often a byproduct of fear, and that must be coming from somewhere. So if you find yourself counting on one deal, a deal so paramount that you can think of nothing else—look out! My guess is that your basket is at risk.

Given my shocking and first-hand experience on the subject, I have devised a simple two-question test that will help any sales rep approaching the irrational obsession stage:

1. *Why am I waiting for this deal?* Chances are, you have let the control for the next step reside with your customer. That means that your customer now has the ball in their court. Talk about your freedom! They can delay for months, or maybe bring in new competition, or just reopen the whole issue to look for new and exciting ways of solving it. All the while you wait, and the basket weakens.

2. *What do I gain by my obsession?* Well, everything, if your obsession is helping you think through an action plan that will bring this deal to a happy end. However, if you are just "stewing," then your obsession is nothing less than self-destruction. It accomplishes nothing except putting a strain on your emotional and physical well-being. Based on my own experience, I would suggest that you get your derriere out the door and work on other hunting and farming activities. If nothing else, distractions from your obsession will help you keep your sanity.

If you're still obsessed and still waiting, then at least take some free advice to preserve what sanity remains: Go and find some more eggs!

## In Review

Obsessing over one opportunity—the one that will make you a hero and endear you to your vice-president—is not good for your emotional well-being. Moreover, putting all your eggs in one basket puts you in a difficult situation if you lose the sale and have nothing to fall back on.

# 77. The World Will Always Be Changing

*"I'll be glad when they finish the management shuffle and things get back to normal!"*

This news flash just in—*the world is changing!* Well, thanks for the tip. I never would have guessed it!

Sarcasm aside, it amazes me how obsessed we've become with the concept of change. Why is that? Alvin Toffler told us back in 1970 that our obsession with change was based on fear. Not the fear of change, per se, but rather the fear of uncertainty that change brings into our life (*Strategic Selling*®–Miller Heiman).

There is an ever-increasing rate of change that is affecting our lives, and consequently we live with growing uncertainty. (I recommend Toffler's first book that was way ahead of its time, *Future Shock*. If you want something more current on the subject, see Toffler's *The Third Wave* or the works of Fullen, Drucker, Mullins, or Rudduck, to mention a few.)

I bring this topic to bear because the corporate sales world is a living study in continuous change, and that means you have to deal with a lot of uncertainty. And I would wager, that while you have little or no control over external change, you do have control over the affect that it has on you. Allow me to introduce the concept of the "human compass."

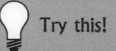 **Try this!**

I challenge you to define your compass. (I highly recommend one of my favorite books—Stephen Covey's The Seven Habits of Highly Effective People—to help you with this task.) In other words, what are the values, standards, ethics, etc. that guide you when facing this mad and ever-changing world of ours?

When you have finished, use this work as a basis to create your own personal mission statement (once again, Stephen Covey's book can help you do this). Your mission statement is the heart of your compass. Feel free to review it often, and make changes as needed (I do!). I have found that when I get caught up in change, I can lose my direction and focus (and my perspective!). At that point I know it's time to pull out my trusty compass (always close by) and that helps me put it all back in perspective—to get my feet back on the ground, if you will. Try it!

Your compass is your guide. It's made up of your standards, your ethics, your values, your morals, and other factors that relate only to you! Naturally, the strength of your compass is a function of your own self-image. If you believe in who you are, what you stand for, and where you're going in life—well, then you have a strong compass. And a strong compass will guide you when powerful external changes come at you from every direction.

I have found that strong-compass people remain relatively calm in the middle of rapid change. They don't ignore change, but rather they explore it. They look at change as another avenue to get where they are going. In a way, life's changes become less about fear, and more about opportunity.

So here's a question: How would you rate your compass? Is there anything you can do to strengthen it? Or perhaps it just needs a little shaking up or dusting off. One thing's for sure—you need it now more than ever because *the only constant in life is change!*

## IN REVIEW

Change is a constant. It's not going away. Increasingly, an individual's capacity to roll with the punches (accept and/or adapt to change) is an important contributor to their personal success (and mental health). An individual's compass—the values, standards, and ethics that one lives by—can play an important role in giving one a solid grounding in which to survive and thrive in the constant changes of our "external" world.

# 78. Waiting by the Phone Will Stop It From Ringing

*"It must be month-end—half the team is sitting by the phone."*

I believe this one falls under "a watched pot never boils."

The best thing that you can do when you're waiting for an important call from a customer is leave the building and occupy yourself elsewhere, or stay at your desk but immerse yourself in a myriad of activities so that you are oblivious to the mere existence of your phone.

Why?

Because you will go out of your mind waiting for that important phone call! No matter how much your customers say they want you—no matter how many times you get a "good feeling" from them—they will never call you with a "yes" when you think they will, and the more you wait, the longer it will take.

Now I realize that I may sound a little superstitious, but I have a little news for you. A consortium of extremely important people did an exhaustive study with unusually scientific measures and concluded, without fear of contradiction, that *the phone never rings when you want it to!*

Part

18

Closing Thoughts

# 79. Earn the Right—Earn the Sale

*"You can't ask him that! You haven't earned the right!"*

"Earning the right" is an expression that salespeople have been using for years, but what does it really mean, and when do you know that you have really "earned the right"?

Easy. Earning the right is basically proving to your customer that you've done what it takes. You earn the right to call an initial meeting. You earn the right to a follow-up meeting. You earn the right to make a presentation, or you earn the right to meet with the big kahuna. And, of course, at the end of the day, you earn the right to ask for the order.

Figuring out whether you've reached this lofty status is actually not that difficult. Here's a simple test—I like to call it a "gut check"—that you can use at any point in a sales cycle. Ask yourself: "Do I deserve to be here?" or "Is the customer in the same place that I am?" or "Have I done the all of the work that I need to do?"

You don't need to do a lot of heavy analysis here—your gut will tell you!

I can recall one sales meeting where my gut was really nagging at me. Despite mild opposition, I was really pushing a customer to sign an order, mainly because of a sales contest that I was vying to win. Somehow, I don't think that my need for the new barbecue was on a par with my customer's need to get the right product. It's funny. It was times

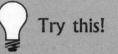

## Try this!

Pick an account that qualifies as a "closable"—meaning that the next logical step is closing the sale. Now, imagine that you are the decision-maker for that sale. What would have to happen between then and now in order for you to say yes and sign the paperwork? The answer to that question is the stuff that you have to do in order to earn the right. So, get to it!

like this that my gut would pipe up and say: "Hey! Junior! Who are we trying to kid here? We've got more work to do, so stop pushing for something that isn't there yet!"

This was one of those times. So, there I sat in front of my customer, mouth agape, listening to my gut whining and complaining while I was privately admitting that my gut was right. I was asking for something that I didn't deserve. But now what do I do? I was in the middle of a close! In this case, I turned to one of the most important of all of the selling proverbs: When all else fails, ask your customer: "Tell me, what do you think is our next logical step here?" (End of story.)

In contrast, reaching the *"right has been earned, proceed as planned"* gut-check status is a really good feeling. I would argue that apart from really big commission or bonus checks, earning the right is probably the most satisfying aspect of selling. And what makes it especially rewarding is the instantaneous change in your customer's behavior at the exact moment that your "right" has been earned. It's that strange but important transition that occurs when your customer begins to really trust you! And you know, that's what earning the right really means. From that moment on, observe as customers stop talking to you like an outsider and begin treating you like one of their own. Watch how they actually return your phone messages (promptly!) and notice how they sincerely ask for your opinion. Then, of course, there's the ultimate: The customer calls you to set up the closing appointment. (Oh, what a feeling!)

A friend of mine once demonstrated the "earn the right" principle better than I ever could. His biggest customer actually assigned a desk and phone to him right down the hall from his own office. Picture the look on a competitor's face when the customer says: "We do business with Mark and his firm and, if you like, you can go and talk to Mark personally. We gave him an office just down the hall!"

Only you will know when you have earned the right!

## IN REVIEW

"Earning the right" means that you deserve to move to the next logical step in the buying process. It means that your customers trust you, and that you're both on the same page of the selling process.

# 80. It's Always the Seller's Responsibility (Excuses Are a Waste of Breath)

*"When the system goes down I just leave a nasty voice mail for my sales rep. She was the one who sold me on reliability, so let her figure it out!"*

Whether we care to admit it, the role of selling carries with it a unique responsibility. It may not be in your job description and it may not be rewarded in cash or bonuses. It may actually be frowned upon by those who just don't understand the true nature of your role, but make no mistake, it's out there.

*Salespeople are responsible for their customers' happiness!*

Ouch! The words bring an aching familiarity. How many unhappy customers have we encountered? (Arguably all of them at one time or another.) How many hours have we spent in post-sale support, exasperated by the knowledge that "Someone else should be fixing this mess. I should be out selling." How many times has our entire well-planned day gone to hell in a handbasket because we were dragged into one customer issue after another? And how many times (this hurts) have we had to look after a major customer-satisfaction issue because there was simply no one else around to do it?

Ah, sad stories, but true.

There's just no escaping it. One of the reasons that few people understand the true challenge of becoming a high-performing sales representative is that salespeople have the awesome responsibility of making and keeping their customers happy. And that isn't well known outside sales circles.

Okay, now a few reality checks.

First, it's okay that it is our responsibility. Put yourself in the customer's shoes. The last thing you would want is a thousand phone numbers to sort through in the middle of a crisis. After all, anyone with common sense knows that when the you-know-what hits the fan, you are going to call the person who has a vested interest in fixing it—the person whose commissions are riding on the sale, the person who made all of the promises and gave all of the assurances, the person whom you know the best—the salesperson, of course.

Second, you can manage the situation if you manage the expectation.

Customers will not call you if they think there is a consistently faster and easier way to fix their problems. I mean, who's kidding whom? Customers are not out to get you; they just want their problems fixed—pronto.

So here's a tip. Just before you dash out their door with a signed order in hand, spend a few valuable moments setting expectations. Explain how your company will deliver on your promises, and be realistic. We all know that brochures and advertisements are not "real world." Every sale on earth is fraught with hiccups, downtime, quality issues, etc., and if something can go wrong, it probably will. So let your customer know about the bad along with the good. Chances are they won't be as enraged when the inevitable problems crop up. But don't stop there! Set accurate performance expectations with your customer, and then continue with a plan for who will support the sale now that the selling is done. If possible, have a "post-sale support rep" of sorts— that's the one person in your organization who will work to get things right, and who will also be there when things go wrong (see also Chapter 49, "Don't Spend Too Much Time Fighting Fires"). Your customers will be relieved to know that their new contact is far more accessible than you. (*"Your post-sale support rep is at their desk, ready to respond to your issues."*)

But wait, that's not all. Before you leave your customer, make sure that you give them the finishing touch, the final peace of mind. Let them know that when all else fails, you will be there to pick up the pieces and make everybody happy again. You'll do this because you know the responsibility for your customer's happiness *rests with you!*

# 81. "Plan-Do-Review" Will Accelerate Your Growth

*"Well, that was an interesting call. Let's talk about it!"*

"Plan-Do-Review" was a way of life at Xerox. It's one of the many concepts that has followed me around into virtually every aspect of my life. We've covered many aspects of the "Plan" and "Do" components in previous chapters, so let's talk about the "Review."

I have a little experiment for you. The next time you finish up an important meeting or telephone call, go out for a coffee—just you, alone with your coffee and your thoughts. Ask yourself: "Okay, what went well there? What was the best part of that call?"

Then ask yourself, "What didn't go so well? If I had a chance to do the call over again, what one thing would I change?"

I would suggest that if that little experiment helps you change the way you approach your next call, or reinforce the things that you are already doing well, then it was worth the time spent and the price of a cup of coffee.

Make this exercise a habit. Write down "Plan-Do-Review" in your day planner or on a card taped to your computer so that it is always in sight. It won't take long before call reviews are almost second nature. For me, they're automatic. After each sales call of any kind, a quick review will help me take a good hard look at my own strengths and weaknesses. I have accepted the fact that my life is a "work in progress."

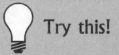 **Try this!**

Upon completing your next call, take a 60-second timeout before letting your mind drift to the next sales activity in your lineup. In those mere 60 seconds, play back the mental recording of that call. Think about what was said and what was done—and maybe what wasn't said or done. Now, listen to your gut and be honest with yourself: "What is the best thing I did during that call? What is the one thing I should do differently?" That's all there is to it. Do not analyze it to death or risk taking needed focus away from your immediate job. Examine just one strength and one area for improvement and you will accelerate your learning curve without even realizing it!

Now, if heavy self-analysis is just not your bag, try the scaled-down version. Ask yourself: "What went well there and what didn't?" In the time it takes you to ride down the elevator, I'm sure that you could come up with at least one good idea to improve your skills. Take the time to review your own performance. I'm here to tell you, the only one who is going to make you better is *you*.

## In Review

We hear a lot about planning and a lot about execution, but what about reflection and review? Taking the time to review calls is a great way to accelerate and reinforce your learning and growth.

# 82. The Sales Rep Is the Sale

*"This product is so good, it will sell itself!"*

Never underestimate the importance of the individual. Nothing gets sold by itself. No matter how inventive your product, or reliable your service, somebody has to find a customer who will buy it.

That somebody is the sales rep.

There have been times in my past when I would get apprehensive just before walking into a customer's office for the first time. I would nervously think to myself: "Another company, another rejection! What am I doing here?"

If you are ever in that situation, a situation of self-doubt and low self-esteem, take a moment to look around the customer's office. Everything in it—every stick of furniture, every picture on the wall, every phone on every desk—was bought and sold!

Customers need salespeople. Customers need you!

Good luck, and good selling!

# Afterword

Reading a book is all well and good, but at the end of the day it is your ownership of personal growth and change that will dictate your success. Otherwise, your reading effort falls into the category of "general interest," which isn't going to drive improved sales results.

So I would like to offer up an official challenge to you, the reader. (I've always wanted to write that!)

## THE CHALLENGE

1. Flip back through the chapters of this book.
2. Think of the one, two, or even three ideas that had the most meaning for you.
3. Figure out how you will apply the idea or skill to a specific selling situation that you're working on (or just use the exercises that have been written for you).
4. Open up your day planner or palm pilot and schedule your improvement.

High-performance sellers learn by doing.

# Index

Operations, selling to, 91-92

# P

Partnership, a sales agreement
    as a, 155-157
Perception, reality and, 255-256
Persistence, 60-61
Personality, 63
Personality, adapting your sales
    skills to fit your, 63-64
Personality, sales, 62-65
Physical appearance, 71-72
Pipeline, 12
Pitch, sales, 45-46
"Plan-Do-Review", 277-278
Planning, 77-78
Politics, company, 152-154
Preparation, lack of, 78
Problem-solving model, 50-51
Problem-solving model, applying,
    51-52
Problem-solving, 49-53
Product, what's important about
    your, 187-189
Proposals, 194-196

# Q

Questioning, interrogator's style,
    27-28
Questions,
    hard-to-ask, 27
    the use of, 25-26

# R

Rackham, Neil, 124, 193, 204, 234
Reality, perception and, 255-256

Recognition, 73
Reference selling, 107-108
Reputation, 103-106
Rewards, 73-74
    motivation for, 74
Ruddock, 265

# S

Sales agreement as a
    partnership, 155-157
Sales call, setting expectations
    for, 47-48
Sales personality,
    creating a, 62-65
Sales skills, adapting to your
    personality, 63-64
Salespeople
    as farmers, 85-87
    as hunters, 85-87
    negative stereotypes about, 45
    skills of successful, 18
    unsuccessful, 12
Sanchez, Diane, 157
*Seinfeld,* 109
Self-confidence, 67-70
Seller, a peddler vs. a, 16-17
Sellers, solution, 95-98
Selling cycle, 39-41
Selling,
    negotiation vs., 231-234
    reference, 107-108
    the role of follow up in,
        136-137
    the true meaning of, 12
    value chain, 168-172
    what it isn't, 14
Servicing, 163-164, 165-167

# About the Author

Terry Beck is Regional Sales Manager for Momentum Systems Ltd., an e-commerce data communications company based in Moorestown, New Jersey. He is also an independent sales performance consultant, helping sales organizations improve their results. He has extensive background in sales, sales management, and sales training and development, and has worked with several Fortune 100 companies including Bell Canada, Bell Mobility, and Xerox Canada, where he was National Sales Trainer and winner of the President's Club and Sales Rep of the Year awards. Born and raised in Canada, Terry and his wife Stacey now make Wilmington, Delaware, their home.